Social Credit Philosophy

Social Credit Philosophy

Our new philosophy will change the run of the universe at once.[1]

---

[1] C.H. Douglas, *The Policy of a Philosophy* (Vancouver: The Institute of Economic Democracy, 1977), 11.

Social Credit Philosophy

ISBN-13: 978-1530390922
ISBN-10: 1530390923

International Academy of Philosophy Press

Irving TX • Gaflei FL
Santiago de Chile • Granada Spain

For more information on Social Credit, please visit the website of the Clifford Hugh Douglas Institute for the Study and Promotion of Social Credit: www.socred.org.

Contents

Acknowledgements   vii

Foreword (by Dr. Josef Seifert)   ix

Author's Preface   xiii

Chapter One: 1
The Basic Philosophical Presuppositions of Social Credit Thought

Chapter Two: 13
The Philosophical Anthropology of Social Credit

Chapter Three: 27
Douglas' Philosophy of Action

Chapter Four: 63
The Social Philosophy of Social Credit

Chapter Five: 99
Social Credit and the 'Philosophy' Underlying the Christian Revelation

Bibliography   111

Index   113

Acknowledgements

In writing this text and preparing it for publication, there are a number of individuals and associations that have offered valuable assistance in one form or another.

A couple of years ago, Wally Klinck read this particular section of my on-going Social Credit research and provided me with some useful feedback. Since then, the text has also been vetted by Chas. Pinwill and Will Waite.

Professor Josef Seifert, my *Doktorvater*, has been kind enough to write the foreword. My philosophical training, which was largely undertaken under Dr. Seifert's supervision at the International Academy of Philosophy (Liechtenstein), was an essential preliminary for the kind of systematic analysis of C.H. Douglas' thought which I have sought to deliver in this present work. Realist phenomenology and Social Credit have many points of contact, and so my early immersion in this particular philosophical school had a priming effect, rendering me even more receptive when I eventually came across Douglas' writings at a later stage. I therefore owe more to Dr. Seifert and to the tradition of phenomenological realism than any specific or tangible benefit that I might cite in connection with this book.

Finally, I must make special mention of my Australian associates and sponsors whose moral and financial support have made such a time-consuming and laborious project as this possible. The Jacaranda tree on the front cover was photographed near Somerset Dam in Queensland in the fall of 2015. I have placed it there as a way of doffing my hat to my friends in the antipodes. It is also symbolic of at least four of the key concepts in Social Credit theory: abundance, balance, respect for the organic, and true freedom. May the Social Credit message, through the tireless efforts of many supporters (both known and unknown) take up its proper place in the public discourse and become efficacious in the moulding of public policy.

Foreword

It is a pleasure for me to briefly introduce this interesting work of the excellent, young philosopher Oliver Heydorn.

Dr. Heydorn was a student of mine for a number of years at the International Academy of Philosophy and successfully defended his doctoral dissertation "Insight and Existence: The Role of *A Priori* Knowledge in the *Cogito* According to Dietrich von Hildebrand" under my guidance.

After applying his philosophical skills and talents to an exploration of the economic theory of Social Credit in *Social Credit Economics,* and to the positive relationship existing between it and Catholic doctrine in *The Economics of Social Credit and Catholic Social Teaching,* he has now turned his attention to an examination of the philosophy lying behind Social Credit.[2]

If there is a recurring message in this book, it is that Social Credit theory, the brainchild of the British engineer Major C.H. Douglas (1879-1952), was firmly established on the foundation of Douglas' *philosophical* realism. While not a professional philosopher himself, Douglas' firmly believed that there is an objective reality, that this reality is governed by laws, and that both the facts of being and its laws are intelligible – however imperfectly and incompletely – to the human mind. This shows the close connection existing between Social Credit and the more enduring contributions to the Western philosophical tradition.

Beyond this, Douglas' emphasis on the priority of the given as the test of truth-claims brings him into close proximity with what I, at any rate, regard as the pinnacle of philosophical achievement in our own times: phenomenological realism. Initiated at the University of Göttingen by Edmund Husserl's *Logical Investigations*[3] in the very early years of the twentieth century, and further developed by various thinkers such as

---

[2] A very complementary review of Heydorn's tome on Social Credit economics may be found on-line here:
http://www.socred.org/index.php/blogs/view/a-review-of-social-credit-economics

[3] Cf. Edmund Husserl, *Logical Investigations*, transl. J. N. Findlay, (London: Routledge & Keegan Paul, 1970); especially *Logische Untersuchungen*. Text der ersten und zweiten Auflage, Bd I: Prolegomena zu einer reinen Logik, hrsg.v. E. Holenstein, Husserliana, Bd. xviii (Den Haag: M. Nijhoff, 1975).

Adolf Reinach,[4] Dietrich von Hildebrand,[5] Roman Ingarden,[6] Saint Edith Stein, and many others, phenomenological realism is, above all, a method or way of doing philosophy.

Knowledge is not a construction or some kind of creation, but is rather a disclosing of what is already present in the world before us. In the act of cognition, the human intellect has the capacity to reach, in a self-transcending contact, the things themselves as they are in themselves.[7] The general methodological approach and analytic tools developed by realist phenomenologists enable us to see clearly what is given in experience, to grasp the states of affairs that are grounded in the objects of consciousness, and to differentiate both from the neighbouring data with which they may be easily confused. In effect, phenomenological realism aims to put philosophy on a sound basis so that Douglas' expressed wish regarding the content of philosophical systems might be fulfilled:

It is very much better that philosophies should follow facts than that facts should be constrained in accordance with philosophies.[8]

---

[4] Especially Adolf Reinach, "The Apriori Foundations of the Civil Law," transl. by J. F. Crosby, *Aletheia* III (1983), pp. xxxiii-xxxv; 1-142; 'Concerning Phenomenology,' transl. from the German ("Über Phänomenologie") by Dallas Willard, *The Personalist* 50 (Spring 1969), pp. 194-221. Reprinted in *Perspectives in Philosophy*, ed. Robert N. Beck (New York: Holt, Reinhart, & Winston, 1961 and 1969).

[5] Especially Dietrich von Hildebrand, *Che cos'è la filosofia?/What Is Philosophy?*, 4th ed., English-Italian (Milano: Bompiani Testi a fronte, 2001), and *Ethics*, 2nd edn (Chicago: Franciscan Herald Press, 1978), *Prolegomena*; the same author, „Das Cogito und die Erkenntnis der realen Welt", Teilveröffentlichung der Salzburger Vorlesungen Hildebrands: 'Wesen und Wert menschlicher Erkenntnis', *Aletheia* 6/1993-1994 (1994), 2-27.

[6] Especially Roman Ingarden, *The Literary Work of Art*, transl. by George G. Grabowicz (Evanston: Northwestern University Press, 1973); see also Josef Seifert, *Discours des Méthodes. The Methods of Philosophy and Realist Phenomenology*, (Frankfurt / Paris / Ebikon / Lancaster / New Brunswick: Ontos-Verlag, 2008).

[7] See Josef Seifert, *Back to Things in Themselves. A Phenomenological Foundation for Classical Realism*, in: "Studies in Phenomenological and Classical Realism." (Boston and London: Routledge and Keegan Paul, 1987), 364 pp., *republished as an e-book* and on paper, August 2013); the same author, "The Receptive Transcendence of Knowledge and the 'Fourth Cogito': Towards a Content-full Notion of 'Early Phenomenology'." *Journal of East-West-Thought* (JET). Spring Number 1, Vol. 4, March 2014, 1-26.

[8] C.H. Douglas, *Warning Democracy*, 3rd ed. (London: Stanley Nott, 1931), 201.

Taking all of these points into consideration, it may be that Douglas' thinking, and therefore Social Credit thought in general, is best described as a kind of "practical philosophy", i.e., as an attempt to bring the institutions and laws that regulate social behaviour into alignment with the natural laws of the universe. The only alternative to proper alignment being chronic social dysfunction and the risk of eventual societal collapse.

I am also struck by the deep personalism of Social Credit thinking. For Douglas, the individual deserves to be affirmed as an end in himself and ought never to be treated as a mere means for the benefit of any group or collective. Perhaps the most succinct formulation of this basic personalistic principle *in relation to social questions* is to be found in Douglas' first book, *Economic Democracy*:

Systems were made for men, and not men for systems.[9]

Not surprisingly, there are also a number of important links and points of contact between Douglas' philosophy and the social teachings of the Christian religion. Heydorn demonstrates that various passages from the New Testament provide a programme for a humane social order that clearly coincides with the spirit of the Social Credit proposals. Douglas has, in fact, succeeded in developing a Christian approach to questions of money and power that stands against all anti-Christian philosophies and policies that are destructive of the common good and individual freedom. In this respect, Douglas' general attitude is very much akin to that of John Paul II who, through his own philosophical/theological reflection and unofficial patronage of the *Solidarność* movement, made a decisive contribution to the overthrow of the communist system in Poland and other parts of Eastern Europe.[10]

---

[9] C.H. Douglas, *Economic Democracy*, 5th ed. (Sudbury, England: Bloomfield Publishers, 1974), 29.

[10] See Pope John Paul II, *Laborem exercens*. See also Rocco Buttiglione, *A Philosophy of Freedom: the Thought of Karol Wojtyła*, Introduction by Michael Novak, Trans. and Afterword by Paolo Guietti and Francesca Murphy (Washington, D.C.: Catholic University of America Press, 1997).

May this work achieve a well-deserved success and contribute to the social and economic well-being of our society!

Josef Seifert,
Dietrich von Hildebrand Chair of Realist Phenomenology
at The International Academy of Philosophy - Instituto de Filosofía Edith Stein (IAP-IFES) in Granada, Spain

Author's Preface

This book is dedicated to an exposition of the central claims that distinguish the more purely *philosophical* dimensions of Social Credit thought. As such, *Social Credit Philosophy* fills a lacuna in the available literature. For neither the founder of Social Credit, Major C.H. Douglas, nor any of his close collaborators, ever endeavoured to publish a systematic account of the philosophical positions and arguments that undergird Social Credit doctrine.

In what follows, I have sought to provide a faithful reconstruction and, where appropriate, an amplification of Douglas' philosophical thinking. *Social Credit Philosophy* is, above all else, a reference text that should be of great use to the serious student. One word of caution, however: while we unfold, in its broad outlines, Major Douglas' general philosophical orientation, no attempt will be made either to provide a complete synopsis of the underlying philosophical theory, or to defend that theory to the extent to which it deserves. There are two reasons for this apparent reticence. To begin with, Douglas did not develop his philosophical views to the same degree as he did when presenting his various positions on economic and political matters. Secondly, since philosophy is, by its very nature, the most open-ended and unbounded of intellectual pursuits, a complete elucidation and defence of Social Credit's philosophical basis would go far beyond the scope of this present work.

A general familiarity with Douglas' philosophical *prise de position* is not a matter of mere academic interest; rather, it is of crucial importance for achieving a proper understanding of his economic, political, and historical ideas. In an address to a conference of Social Crediters in London in 1937, Douglas underscored the importance of philosophy for Social Credit in the following terms:

> [I]t is a very superficial definition of Social Credit that it is merely a scheme of monetary reform; ...
>
> Social Credit is the policy of a philosophy. It is something based on what you profoundly believe — what at any rate, I profoundly believe, and hope you will — to be a portion of reality. It is probably a very small portion, but we have glimpsed a portion of reality, and that conception of reality is a philosophy, and the action that we take

based upon that conception is a policy, and that policy is Social Credit. It is in fact a policy based upon a philosophy, which is, incidentally, why, in many cases, it is no use arguing with many people about the technics of Social Credit, because they don't agree with your philosophy; often they don't even understand it, and, therefore, what you say in regard to policy and technics sounds like a loud noise to them, chiefly without any sense; and the best thing to do in the circumstance is, of course, to agree to differ.[11]

In other words, Douglas' diagnoses of our economic, political, and cultural ills, as well as the policies and mechanisms that he suggested for their rectification, all presupposed a specific point of view, a vision of what the world is like and how we can and ought to behave in relation to it if we are to obtain all that we fundamentally and rightfully desire from our various associations. He was convinced, and with reason, that the Social Credit 'glimpse of reality', while incomplete (in the sense of being primarily focused on just one aspect of our experience: the social power of human beings working in association), was nevertheless of cardinal importance because it bore the mark of truth and was also deeply practical in its implications :

All that you can say about Social Credit, either in its monetary aspects, or in these aspects I am discussing to-night, is that we see — and I profoundly believe that we do see — just a little bit of the way in which the universe does in fact act.[12]

Every human association, every organization of individuals into groups, generates an unearned increment in the form of social power, what we refer to in Social Credit theory as the 'social credit' (without capitals). This power can be directed toward the achievement of various ends. The fulfillment of some of these ends redounds to the satisfaction of the individuals who comprise the association on a fair and equitable basis, while the pursuit of other ends undermines the association by involving its members (usually against their knowledge

---

[11] C.H. Douglas, *The Policy of a Philosophy* (Vancouver: The Institute of Economic Democracy, 1977), 3.

[12] Ibid., 10.

and/or will and always at their illegitimate expense) in the realization of anti-social objectives for the benefit of an oligarchic few. Douglas' social philosophy explains both why and how it is that associations often fail to serve their fundamental or true purposes as well as they might, and it also reveals what should be done in terms of re-habilitation. For what Douglas discovered was something that is often taken for granted but rarely, if ever, properly formulated as an abiding axiom for our guidance: there is only one basis for the establishment of a stable and flourishing association: effective co-operation in the ser-vice of the common will.

Chapter One: The Basic Philosophical Presuppositions of Social Credit Thought

Before we proceed to embark on a close examination of their more specific and defining content, it will be advantageous to properly contextualize Social Credit's philosophical underpinnings by briefly surveying their overarching parameters.

Douglas' Definition of Philosophy

There is a potential source of confusion which stems from how C.H. Douglas used the noun 'philosophy' which must be eliminated right from the outset. Like 'social credit', 'philosophy' is a paronymous term which may designate any one of several closely related phenomena. It may refer to the academic discipline, to a specific body of doctrines which comprises the product of someone's philosophical reflection, or else to a certain manner of analyzing and evaluating things, i.e., to a special form of investigation or inquiry.

Along the lines of the second of the aforementioned meanings, Major Douglas once defined philosophy quite broadly as any body of thought which constitutes a general "conception of reality".[13] It seems that what Douglas had in mind is something much more extensive than the 'conception of reality' which philosophy understood in the strictest of senses, i.e., as the eidetic analysis of the core or heart of reality, is in a position to deliver, and that what he actually intended under the term 'philosophy' is something more akin to *Weltanschauung* or 'worldview'.[14] For Douglas, 'philosophy' refers to a propositional picture of reality as whole, or some particular aspect of it. Such a vision of reality may contain, in addition to strictly philosophical truth-claims, theological, scientific, and historical components, etc. Through-

---

[13] C.H. Douglas, *The Policy of a Philosophy* (Vancouver: The Institute of Economic Democracy, 1977), 3.

[14] By 'eidetic analysis', I am referring to the cognition of the necessary and universal states of affairs that are grounded in essential necessities, what realist phenomenology refers to as necessary essences and relations.

1

out the remainder of the text, the term 'philosophy' will be placed in single quotation marks whenever it is used in this special sense.

As far as Social Credit is concerned, the significance of a *Weltan-schauung* lies in the fact that in trying to orient the thinking or beha-viour of an individual or a group of people, one must assume an intellectual picture of what reality is like as one's point of departure. Within such a 'conception of reality', the most important elements would involve propositions concerning the nature of man, the nature of the universe, the nature of man's relationship with that universe, the nature of his relationship to his fellows, and the meaning/purpose of his existence, etc. In other words, there is an *Orientierungsphilosophie* or orientational philosophy which lies at the bottom of every *Weltanschau-ung*.

Naturally, not all worldviews are of equal value. Some are closer to truth because they correspond to a greater degree to the objective na-ture of reality, while others are further away from truth because they present a picture which significantly deviates from that reality. This implies that the usefulness of a *Weltanschauung* in providing individu-als with a reliable guide for thought and action, one that enables them to achieve intended results, is a function of the truth-value that might be attached to that *Weltanschauung*.

The General Philosophical Orientation of Social Credit

Speaking of philosophy in the narrower and more correct sense (i.e., as a search for the basic and unchanging principles that define and delimit reality), it is important to recognize that the analysis and remedial pro-posals of Social Credit's economic and political theory are grounded in a general philosophical outlook which has much in common with what is often referred to as the *philosophia perennis*.[15]

---

[15] The *philosophia perennis* encompasses that broad tradition of thought in the history of Western philosophy which insists on the existence of objective reality and its basic in-telligibility to the human mind. Its major figures include Socrates, Plato, Aristotle, St. Augustine, Boethius, and St. Thomas Aquinas, amongst many others.

Philosophical Realism

Consider, for example, the fact that the underlying philosophical orientation of Social Credit unmistakably entails a metaphysical, epistemological, and methodological realism.[16] On the occasion of his address to the Constitutional Research Association, Douglas made the epistemological and metaphysical realism of his thinking quite clear:

> **The justification, if any, which I should advance for my temerity in addressing an audience of such wide and distinguished qualifications both in Statesmenship and Law, is that I am concerned with what appears to be a somewhat neglected point of view – objective reality. I do not think we realise the extent to which Absolute Idealism, to use its technical name, has tinctured thinking on this subject – that nothing exists outside the mind of the beholder and that, for instance, totalitarian Government only requires mass propaganda to be just as good and much easier, than any other variety. Put quite shortly, my main thesis is that this is not true; that the rules of the Universe transcend human thinking, and cannot, in the ordinary sense of the words, be altered, and therefore must be**

---

[16] In an article which appeared on his blog entitled "Social Credit and Existentialism", Albertan Social Crediter Jim Schroeder has argued that, as a matter of fact, the underlying philosophy of Social Credit is not realism at all but existentialism, cf. http://social-credit. blogspot.com/2008/07/social-credit-and-existentialism.html. Schroeder takes issue with how realism typically defines epistemic truth, i.e., as the conformity of thought with being. He further points out that this way of conceiving truth has the effect of subordinating the individual person to an impossible goal and is therefore antithetical to the Social Credit approach to the problems of life. Insofar as this definition of epistemic truth might be interpreted in an absolutist or totalizing manner, I find myself in complete agreement that any such 'realism' must be rejected both by philosophy and by Social Credit. The truth far exceeds what can be humanly grasped and it should not be reduced without residue nor identified with the correspondence existing between *human* thought and being. In virtue of its finitude, a perfect correspondence between thought and being could never be achieved by any human mind. As Kierkegaard remarked in his *Concluding Unscientific Postscript*, reality could only be a complete system for God, but not for any human person or finite spirit. In describing Douglas' philosophical approach as a form of realism, I wish to make it clear that neither Douglas nor I myself would wish to present the realistic approach as anything other than a *tool* by means of which human beings can obtain the type of technical knowledge which is useful in making intended results concrete realities (amongst other cognitive goals).

ascertained and obeyed.[17]

The claim that the laws of being exist independently of the human mind and need to be both cognized and obeyed revealed Douglas' belief that there is an objective reality and that it can, to at least some extent and however imperfectly, be known by human beings. In keeping with this contention, the journal of Douglas' Social Credit Secretariat, *The Social Crediter*, bore the subheading "For Political and Economic Realism".

The General Nature of Objective Reality

Douglas acknowledged that this reality which exists independently of the human mind bears both a material as well as a spiritual dimension. The tendency of some modern thinkers to reduce all being to the physical, to matter-in-motion, was decried by him because, being a false conception of things, it could not but be productive of harmful consequences:

> **We all know what happens if you put copper wires into a wrong relationship with a powerful electric current, and there is ample evidence to show that our ignorance or disdain of everything but materialism is causing a spiritual "short circuit."**[18]

Competing Schools of Thought - The Nature and Origin of Knowledge

Beyond the debates between realism and some form of idealism and between materialist and non-materialist doctrines, a third perennial issue in the history of philosophy has been the question regarding the origin and consequent nature of human knowledge. In his 1924 book entitled *Social Credit*, Douglas described at some length the antagonism which has always existed in one form or another between the two very different approaches to epistemic justification which have characterized philosophical inquiry (and indeed inquiry in general) and the disorienting effects which these clashing perspectives exert over the modern mind:

---

[17] C.H. Douglas, *Realistic Constitutionalism* (London: K.R.P. Publications Ltd., 1947), 3. The methodological realism of Social Credit will be dealt with at length in a subsequent section.

[18] Ibid., 7.

We have in England, probably to a greater extent than elsewhere, two distinct systems of education flourishing side by side. The distinction is clearly marked in the public schools and universities; but it is traceable through every grade of educational institution by the arrangements which are made to prepare candidates for public and other examinations. These two systems in the Public Schools are the Classical and Modern sides, and have their equivalent Triposes and Honours Schools in the universities.

Now, it does not seem to be so clearly realised as it should be, that these two systems of education are, considered separately, incompatible with each other. The classical system is the embodiment of an extraordinarily attractive and artistic ideal or conception of the nature of society, and the conditions under which society lives, moves, and has its being. It is above, outside, possibly in advance of, facts. The modern school, of which inductive natural science, based upon the experimental ascertainment of fact, is the back-bone, has not essentially anything to do with ideals at all. It is realistic; its first postulate is that forces always act in a similar manner when placed in a similar relation to each other. It refuses to admit, as a fact, anything which cannot be demonstrated, and as a theory, anything which does not fit the facts. For example, the classical ideal contends that men "ought" to be good, brave and virtuous. The modern, that it does not understand the meaning of goodness, that bravery and virtue are not capable of exact definition, and, that so far as the word "ought" has any meaning, it postulates the existence of a force so far undemonstrated.

It will be easily recognised on a moderate consideration, that the effect on the everyday world of these two philosophies cannot fail to be disruptive. The logical outcome of the classical ideal is to lay the emphasis of any observed defects in the social organisation on defects in the characters of the persons composing the society. Wars occur because people are wicked, poverty, because people are idle, crime because they are immoral. Material progress, which in its essence is applied Science, is repulsive to the Classical mind, because it does, in fact, stultify the rigid Classical ideal. Conversely, the scientific attitude tends to the opposite extreme, towards what is called Determinism; that people's actions, thoughts, and morals, are

purely the outcome of more or less blind forces to which they are subjected, and in regard to which, both censure and praise are equally out of place.[19]

The two different approaches to epistemic justification which Douglas described – from the point of view of the two different systems of education which they inspire – are, of course, those of rationalism (which he labelled as the classical school) and empiricism (which he referred to as the modern school). Broadly speaking, rationalism claims that knowledge of the mind-independent world is obtained through the operations of reason, i.e., independently of any experiential contact with that world in this present life.[20] Different 'rationalist' philosophers have developed different ways of explaining the origin of this knowledge, whether it be through *anamnesis* (Plato), innate ideas (Descartes), or divine illumination (Augustine). Empiricism, on the other hand, holds that knowledge of the mind-independent world can only be obtained through the experience of that world, but experience is arbitrarily restricted to sensory or cognate forms of perception.

It should not be at all surprising that, given the opposition inherent in the two positions, rationalist and empiricist approaches to knowledge acquisition have often led, as Douglas duly noted, to incompatible truth-claims in various spheres. Rationalist philosophers tend to affirm the existence of God, the spirituality and freedom of the human person, the objectivity of the moral order, etc., while empiricist philosophers, by contrast, tend to interpret such claims as mere projections of the human imagination that are devoid of any foundation in the given. In other words, one's epistemic orientation would appear in many cases to be correlated with a certain sort of metaphysics, whether or not the latter is to be construed as either the cause or the consequence of the former. How is one to adjudicate between competing truth-claims which are based on such radically different perspectives?

---

[19] C.H. Douglas, *Social Credit* (London: Cecil Palmer, 1924), 2-4.

[20] The 'mind-independent world' refers to the way things are independently of our thinking and/or perception.

Besides decrying the disruptive effect of these two warring 'philo-sophies' on the orientation of individuals and society at large, Douglas expressed in the same section of the book a longing for and indeed an intimation of a *higher synthesis* (which he sensed must be the correct position with respect to this particular issue concerning proper epistemic justification), while tacitly admitting that he was not in a position to deliver this synthesis himself:

> It is very probable that, as in many controversies, there is a good deal to be said for both points of view, but it is even more probable that approximate truth lies in appreciation of the fact that neither con-ception is useful without the other. It is probable that in the less fortunately situated strata of society, a theory of economic Deter-minism would be a sound and accurate explanation for the actions of 98 per cent. of the persons to whom it might be applied; that those persons are, in fact, obliged to act and think in accordance with limitations which are imposed upon them by their environment. In short, that their environment is more powerful in shaping them, than they are in shaping their environment. But this is not true of all of their more fortunate contemporaries. There are, without a doubt, circumstances in the world, in which the personal conceptions of individuals can have powerful and far-reaching consequences on their immediate and even national or continental environment. It seems reasonable to believe that a Napoleon, a Washington, or a Bismarck have, in effect, changed the course of history, just as it is certain that a James Watt, a George Stephenson, or a Faraday, have altered the centre of gravity of industrial and economic society.[21]

As far as the present writer is aware, Douglas had no contact with or even awareness of the realist phenomenology of the Munich and Göt-tingen circles though he lived contemporaneously with all of their major and minor thinkers. Had he enjoyed such contact, he would have been pleased to discover that the higher synthesis for which he longed was actually being developed and, if applied correctly, could be used to help eliminate the disruptive existential and societal effects which attend the

---

[21] C.H. Douglas, *Social Credit* (London: Cecil Palmer, 1924), 4-5.

rationalist-empiricist conflict by placing man's general epistemological orientation on a sounder basis, i.e., one which is more in line with reality.[22] Douglas' implicit position with respect to the rationalist-empiricist debate is only one amongst several points of contact existing between his general philosophical orientation and the school of realist phenomenology. As such, his thinking on this particular controversy places him once again within the broad tradition of the *philosophia perennis*.

Dangers of Rationalism – The Fetishism of Autonomous Reason

Even though he was not a coarse empiricist, Douglas was keen to point out the dangers inherent in the type of mindset which was nourished by the continental rationalism of the 16th and 17th centuries.

Reason, narrowly understood as the power of deductive inference, can be a useful tool but ought not, in any way, to be absolutized as *the* source of knowledge. The problem with the deductive mindset is that the act of deduction is only as adequate as the information contained in the original premises:

> "Reason," as I understand it, is nearly synonymous with logic, of which mathematics is a special example. It is a pure mechanism, just as a slide rule is a mechanism, and as such, is deterministic. You put into the mechanism practically anything you please, and you get out something which was inherent in what you put in, but nothing further. If I say that $(a+b)^2 = a^2 + 2ab + b^2$, I can apply that very useful piece of information to a number of concrete problems, but they must, on each occasion, concern similar objects. It is no use saying that the square of a apples plus b oranges gives you some information about bananas. It does not.[23]

---

[22] Readers who are interested in the solution offered by realist phenomenology to this particular problem, i.e., the grounding of synthetic *a priori* knowledge on an intuitive and experiential contact with being, would to do well to consult Dietrich von Hildebrand's book *What is Philosophy?* 3rd ed. (London and New York: Routledge, 1991). Cf. also, Josef Seifert, *Discours des Méthodes. The Methods of Philosophy and Realist Phenomenology* (Frankfurt: Ontos-Verlag, 2008) and „Was ist Philosophie? Die Antwort der Realistischen Phänomenologie", *Zeitschrift für philosophische Forschung* 49 H 1 (1995), 92-103., as well as Fritz Wenisch, *Die Philosophie und ihre Methode* (Salzburg: A. Pustet, 1976).

[23] C.H. Douglas, *The Realistic Position of the Church of England* (Liverpool: K.R.P. Publications Ltd., 1948), 14-15.

Even if the original premises in an argument happen to be true, the picture which reason deduces will be false in whole or in part if some key piece of information is omitted and this can only be productive of negative consequences:

> **[T]he great danger of placing too much reliance on the deductive method, is that the whole of its conclusions are rendered misleading and dangerous if an essential factor is omitted from the premises.**[24]

Should one adopt a broader understanding of 'reason' to include, for example, the power of rational insight, of constructing hypotheses, of inductive inferences, etc., in addition to deductive inference, one must still never lose sight of the fact that the human intellect is limited and that reality is therefore always far greater than what reason can capture. Reason in this richer sense may well be the supreme power behind the universe, but it is not supremely manifested in human minds. In fact, human reason can only function properly to the extent that it opens itself to reality as the latter gives itself to human cognition; it must be the servant of reality, not the master. The consequence of subordinating reality to or identifying reality with human reason is an idolatrous and faulty intellectualism:

> **One of the results of intellectualism is more or less complete aberration of judgment; what we usually but incorrectly call common sense; a loss of the instinctive valuation of the meaning of things. If the word "intellect" be substituted for "Satan", the phrase "Satan is unchained" is a simple description, as well as an explanation, of the condition in which we find ourselves today, with our "science" which has reduced us to serfdom.**[25]

---

[24] C.H. Douglas, *Social Credit*, rev. ed. (New York: Gordon Press, 1973), 50.

[25] C.H. Douglas, *The Development of World Dominion* (Sydney: Tidal Publications, 1969), 84-85.

In dealing with the subject of the French Revolution and its aftermath, Douglas once made the following observations:

> [T]he distinguishing characteristic of the period under comment is the triumph of the Age of Reason heralded by the intellectuals who were the stalking-horse of the Terror - a triumph the fruits of which are already laden with an unimaginable bitterness. Behind events, persons and Race, there has been active the cult of Lucifer the Light Bringer, and *logic, rationalism,* is the hallmark of that cult.

The problems of the world are not purely intellectual problems; intellect and ultimate good are not one and the same thing.

Dangers of Empiricism – The Fetishism of Natural Science

Alongside the epistemological disorientation that can be provoked by continental rationalism, Douglas likewise acknowledged that empiricism can give rise to its own particular type of cognitive misdirection. There is, in the modern world, a tendency amongst some to unquestioningly regard the practice of empirical science as an undeniable source of objective knowledge about the world. Insofar as science subordinates itself to reality it can indeed discover new facts and verify new hypotheses; all too often, however, reality is forced to fit the theoretical preferences of scientists and facts are left undiscovered, ignored, or misinterpreted. Since the acceptance of scientific claims is a matter of faith for the vast majority of persons who may not have the talent, training, funding, or time to verify every 'discovery' for themselves and since natural scientists, even when they are sincerely seeking answers from reality, do not often clearly distinguish between factual claims and possible theoretical explanations for those facts, all scientific affirmations, whether true or false, tend to be uncritically accepted by many people. "It has been scientifically proven that …" becomes, all too often, a sufficient justification for belief. The scope

---

Only a perverse obscurantism would deny the value of Reason properly regarded, just as it would be fatuous to condemn a slide-rule, with which it has an organic connection, as being in itself reprehensible. But the idea, if it can be so called, that "values" are ultimately physico-mathematical (put forward, *e.g.*, by Sir Edmund Whittaker in the 1948 Herbert Spencer Lecture) seems to us to be a compact instance of the delirium of Idolatry not the less fatal because of its appeal to Rationality.

It is highly significant that the worship of logic is characteristic of immaturity, of youth. At the age of eighteen or so, logic presents an indisputable proof for every problem. And it will be noticed that there has been, and is, a conscious "youth movement" carrying with it the implication that wisdom reaches its apex in the early twenties.

Yet it must be plain to anyone that not only is evidence lacking that logic has solved any political problems of consequence in the past, but, conversely, that the policies now current in world affairs, which pretend to base their appeal on logic, threaten us with destruction.

There is no saying requiring attention more clamantly than "Unless ye become as little children ye shall in no wise enter the Kingdom". There is nothing logical about a little child. Ibid., 78-79.

within this type of epistemological atmosphere for the operation of what is, in fact, pseudo-science is very great indeed.

Like history, and many other fields of inquiry that lie beyond immediate, everyday experience, it must be granted that natural science can also be easily politicized; i.e., the types of scientific claims which are allowed widespread publicity may be those which promise to advance some political (or commercial) agenda, rather than those which are actually true:

> It has been observed in many quarters, and notably by Dr. Tudor Jones, F.R.S.E., that modern science is becoming a mass of superstitions. The tendency of modern, and even not-so-modern Universities to produce communists has been traced to the insistence of their teaching staffs on the unlimited validity of such theories as that of Darwin, largely discredited in informed quarters, but presented to immature minds as fully established.[26]

---

[26] C.H. Douglas, *The Brief for the Prosecution* (Liverpool: K.R.P. Publications Ltd., 1945), 5.

Chapter Two: The Philosophical Anthropology of Social Credit

One of the specific sub-disciplines of philosophy in which Social Credit theory holds and defends substantive claims is that field known as philosophical anthropology or the 'philosophy of the human person'. Given that Social Credit focuses on the nature, conditions, and limits of human association, it must necessarily presuppose definite positions on the key issues that arise in connection with a philosophical examination of human nature and human purpose.

The Social Credit view of Human Nature

The Nature of the Individual

In keeping with the Christian revelation, Social Credit affirms that the human being differs from all other living beings because he possesses, albeit in an analogous and creaturely manner, certain divine characteristics such as rationality and the gift of free will:

> **Although the fact is a little obscured at the moment, the human individual is the highest manifestation of divine attributes with which we are in day-to-day contact. What differentiates him from the lower orders, when he is different, is his initiative – the fact that he manoeuvres under his own steam. I am confident that there is an organised attempt to drive him down the scale of existence, so that he becomes primarily a number on a card index, by taking away as far as possible any recognisable initiative, his potentially divine attribute.[27]**

---

[27] C.H. Douglas, *The Big Idea* (Bullsbrook, Australia: Veritas Publishing Company, 1983), 6. Cf. C.H. Douglas, *The Development of World Dominion* (Sydney: Tidal Publications, 1969), 23: "Almost the highest attribute of man is 'judgment', the exercise of choice. Far more than learning, it moulds the character and shapes the abilities, ..." At the deepest level, however, it would appear that free will is best understood not as the ability to choose between alternatives, but rather as a certain ability (however limited) to act independently of external causes.

Closely connected with rationality and the capacity for making free choices is the ability of the human being to be motivated by those future possibilities which he has merely imagined:

There is a curious faculty in the human make-up – the make-up of the cosmos if you like – which enables it to project forward its ideas, and then to fill those ideas with solid fact.[28]

It is the human being's *creative initiative*, which is grounded in his rationality, imagination, and free will, which makes the human being an *individual* and which differentiates him from the next highest level of being, that of animals. This ontological uniqueness of the human individual bears important implications for the proper or due relation which, in sharp contrast to what occurs amongst animals, should exist between human individuals and the groups or associations in which these individuals are embedded:

[T]he real test of difference between the animal kingdom and the human race is the individuality of the human soul. That is to say, the first "duty" of the human being is to dominate his relationship with the group soul.[29]

Metaphysically speaking, "groups are inferior to individuals"[30] and the

---

[28] C.H. Douglas, *The Monopolistic Idea* (Vancouver: The Institute of Economic Democracy, 1979), 5.

[29] C.H. Douglas, *The Big Idea* (Bullsbrook, Australia: Veritas Publishing Company, 1983), 19.

[30] Ibid., 59. The metaphysical inferiority of groups in comparison with individuals can be demonstrated by considering, in keeping with the scholastic axiom *'actio sequitur esse'*, that individuals are capable of a higher form of life than any group: "Measured by civilised standards, groups are always of lower value than individuals. Conversely, individuals have qualities which are non-existent in groups. I suppose a life-long plot on the part of one man against the well-being of another man is very rare, but a business or national vendetta is the rule, and I should say there were few exceptions to that rule. Acts of generosity without ulterior motive between individuals are common – between nations or businesses as such, are unknown." C.H. Douglas, *Warning Democracy*, 3rd ed. (London: Stanley Nott, 1935), 75. Cf. also, C.H. Douglas, *The Development of World Dominion* (Sydney: Tidal Publications, 1969), 47: "a collectivity has no moral standards of its own, and invariably reflects the lowest morals of its constituent units."

varied relationships existing between individual human beings and their groups should always reflect that fact.

The Inequality of Human Nature

In spite of the high ontological status of the human individual as such (or, better put, precisely because of it), it is necessary to recognize that neither human individuals nor groups of individuals are equal in any comprehensive metaphysical sense as far as the endowments of nature are concerned:

Men and women never were equal, are not equal at the present time, and, in my opinion, never will be equal....[31]

The contradictory belief, i.e., the claim that all human individuals and groups are qualitatively equal, appears to be one of the fruits of the widespread materialism which asserts that everything can be reduced to matter in motion:

The tendency to argue from the particular to the general is a special case of the sequence from materialism to collectivism. If the universe is reduced to molecules, ultimately we can dispense with a catalogue and a dictionary; all things are the same thing, and all words are just sounds – molecules in motion. That is the ultimate meaning of "Equality" – having no quality.[32]

---

[31] C.H. Douglas, *Major C.H. Douglas Speaks* (Sydney: Douglas Social Credit Association, 1933), 38. Cf. C.H. Douglas, *Programme for the Third World War* (Liverpool: K.R.P. Publications Ltd., 1943), 20: "The claim that 'all men are born free and equal,' if anyone makes it, clearly rests, even to be arguable, on the proposition that each new birth is a new individual, *ab initio*. This idea meets with little support nowadays. .... anyone who will spend a little time observing half a dozen babies of about twelve months old must admit wide differences, not to be accounted for by either health or environment. The human infant almost certainly begins a new day with certain individualities, however acquired, ..."

[32] C.H. Douglas, *The Brief for the Prosecution* (Liverpool: K.R.P. Publications Ltd., 1945), preface. In *The Development of World Dominion*, Douglas quoted with approval the following excerpt from an article written by Robert Fordyce Aickman entitled "Quality and Equality": "individualism is the basis of all quality, and can only flourish in freedom. Equality is the great enemy of quality." C.H. Douglas, *The Development of World Dominion* (Sydney: Tidal Publications, 1969), 5.

On the contrary, people are created with different kinds and degrees of talents as well as defects and no two individuals are exactly alike, just as different families, or men and women generally, or the various ethnic and racial groups of mankind are not exactly alike. On account of these differences in attributes and abilities we are invariably confronted with the reality of inequality. For Douglas, the fact of ontological inequality was not seen, however, as something which possessed a negative value, i.e., as something which needed to be destroyed or rectified:

People clamour for equality, although not so much as they used to do, whereas the very last thing the average individual really desires is equality. He is convinced, and in my opinion, properly convinced, that he is quite different to everyone else, and the modern demand to realise one's real personality is far nearer the truth than the clamour for equality of the beginning of the last century.[33]

Inequality is a necessary by-product of authentic individuality and can only increase as people develop themselves and become increasingly different. Rather than trying to standardize human beings so that they match some pre-fit cookie cutter notion of sameness (which would be contrary to the nature of reality because "Individuality demands its own unique relationship to circumstances"[34]), legitimate differences between individuals (those consistent with the functional necessities of associations), including those which entail inequalities of various sorts, should be respected and indeed celebrated. This implies, by extension, that the fact of inequality ought never to be used as an excuse for the exploitative, disrespectful, or otherwise oppressive treatment of any individual or group.[35] On the contrary, each individual should be positively promoted and empowered to develop his own personality to the fullest degree to which

---

[33] C.H. Douglas, *Warning Democracy*, 3rd ed. (London: Stanley Nott, 1935), 23-24.

[34] Ibid., 116.

[35] In connection with this aspect of the subject, Douglas pointed out that the socio-economic inequalities existing under present day economic and political associations should not be uncritically accepted as correct reflections of the underlying metaphysical inequalities which undoubtedly exist amongst human beings:

his nature allows. Such a policy of affirmation could not threaten or destabilize a social structure, provided that that social structure was not built up on the types of artificial scarcities in which contemporary associations wallow. It is the fear of what true respect for genuine diversity would imply, i.e., the loss of centralized control, which is responsible for many of our political problems:

> **The curious self-defeating perversity which fails to see that there is plenty of privilege for everyone, because of the infinite diversity both of people and of opportunity (and that the problem is to let more people get at it not to take it from those who have it), is the perfect tool for the World Planner.**[36]

Heredity as One of the Chief Roots of Inequality

In the debate concerning the roles which nature and nurture play in forming a person's *basic* attributes and capacities, Douglas sided firmly with nature; i.e., the raw material or 'hardware' which the free spiritual person has to work with is primarily determined by the endowments of nature, i.e., by genes and other inherited factors. In his address entitled 'Realistic Constitutionalism' Douglas made the following observation:

"There is, of course, a radical difference between the repudiation of the idea that all men (and women) are equal or are born equal, which seems to me to be demonstrably untrue, and the *non sequitur* that the differences in economic and social status in individuals which exist at the present time are correct reflections of individual differences. They certainly are not. There are 'reincarnation' theories which appear to claim that they are – that every individual has created the circumstances in which he now lives by his actions in the past. Apart from many other objections to this idea in the realm of philosophy, it appears to be logically indistinguishable from determinism."

C.H. Douglas, *Programme for the Third World War* (Liverpool: K.R.P. Publications Ltd., 1943), 20-21.

The same observation could be made *mutatis mutandis* regarding the socio-economic inequalities existing between different nations; i.e., they are not necessarily the isomorphic reflection on the economic, political, and social planes of more fundamental metaphysical inequalities.

[36] C.H. Douglas, *"Whose Service is Perfect Freedom"* (Bullsbrook, Western Australia: 1983), 47-48.

> **Professor Karl Pearson's assistant, Miss Elderton, in "The relative strength of Nature and Nurture," states "Heredity is four times as potent as environment." ... Yet the claims of heredity were never so derided, whether under the cloak of "racism" or class privilege....[37]**

The environment cannot change this underlying human nature, but it can either foster or thwart its various tendencies.[38] In other words, the ontological inequality of human beings is, *in the first place*, a function of their differing biological heritages. At the same time, what one does with this legacy, i.e., whether and to what extent one makes a constructive or destructive use of it, is something which comes under the free control of the spiritual person.[39]

---

[37] C.H. Douglas, *Realistic Constitutionalism* (London: K.R.P. Publications Ltd., 1947), 6.

[38] Cf. C.H. Douglas, *The Realistic Position of the Church of England* (Liverpool: K.R.P. Publications Ltd., 1948), 8: "Governmental systems do not change human nature, but they can, and do foster various aspects of it." Cf., also: C.H. Douglas, *Major C.H. Douglas Speaks* (Sydney: Douglas Social Credit Association, 1933), 46: "What, I think, is incontestably true is that the great underlying forces which inspire human nature to action do not change substantially, at any rate within the widest period of history which we can span, although, like everything else, they may be subject to evolution and they may change their forms of expression."

In consequence, any ideology which claims that it is possible to substantially change human nature by the application of external forces in the environment would, from a Social Credit perspective, have to be rejected as false:

"the ideas being so widely propagated by Marxists and others, that the characteristics of a race, not to say an individual can be revolutionised in a lifetime, are not merely nonsense – they are deadly, dangerous, nonsense.

I do not believe that the individual character is much changed in one lifetime. People become a little wiser, or a little more foolish, a little kinder, or a little harder, a little more reliable or a little less honest. They may and do take veneers, but the real wood changes slowly. I do not believe that there is any ascertainable difference in the Russian of to-day, and the Russian of the Czarist period, other than the disappearance of a travelled and at any rate superficially cultured class who were certainly more decorative."

C.H. Douglas, *Programme for the Third World War* (Liverpool: K.R.P. Publications Ltd., 1943), 21.

[39] From the interaction of nature, environment, and free will, new and even more important layers of inequality can arise. The choices people make in view of the information to which they are exposed can have a significant impact on the development of their personalities.

The Basic Goodness of Human Nature

Whatever its faults, limits, or weaknesses, Douglas also held that human nature is, at bottom, essentially good and that the best thing that can be done in the interests of promoting its flourishing is to mould the environment in such a way that one's inherent potential for a positive and organic development of the personality can be called forth into being in the easiest manner possible.

To this view of human nature, we can, of course, oppose the 'puritan' interpretation of the dogma of original sin, which would lead people to affirm that "it is not good for people to have what they want, that human nature is essentially bad, and that life should consist to a very large extent in running to see what Johnnie is doing, and telling him he mustn't."[40]

It was in reference to this particular *(mis)understanding* of the Christian dogma of original sin that Douglas once asserted: "I do not believe in original sin."[41]

---

[40] C.H. Douglas, *Warning Democracy*, 3rd ed. (London: Stanley Nott, 1935), 27-28. Cf. C.H. Douglas, *The Breakdown of the Employment System* (Vancouver: The Institute of Economic Democracy, 1923), 9: "It [Puritanism - OH] claims that human nature is essentially vile, and can only be kept within bounds by being kept so busy that it has no time to get into mischief."

[41] C.H. Douglas, *The Nature of Democracy* (Vancouver: The Institute of Economic Democracy, 1934), 5. This particular explanation for Douglas' apparent denial of the dogma is confirmed by his own words in the very same speech in which the apparent denial occurs: "It is, of course, possible to contend that the desires of a mob [in this particular context, Douglas made it clear that the 'mob' simply means 'the people'; 'mob' was not being used pejoratively – OH] are always or frequently wrong. That is the blasphemy based on the theory of original sin, which is evident in the world to-day in various forms which can be largely included in the word "Puritanism"." Ibid, 5.. In a later lecture, *The Realistic Position of the Church of England*, Douglas admitted that there is a legitimate meaning to the dogma of original sin, i.e., one which corresponds to reality: "It is not necessary to go outside the experience of an ordinary lifetime to learn that the doctrine of original sin has a real meaning, ..." C.H. Douglas, *The Realistic Position of the Church of England* (Liverpool: K.R.P. Publications Ltd., 1948), 9. This legitimate meaning can be identified with the Catholic understanding of the dogma; i.e., in spite of the fact that human beings are vulnerable to evil impulses because, *inter alia*, the will is weak and the intellect often clouded, human nature remains essentially good: "No experienced individual is a starry-eyed idealist about human nature – its qualities range from far infra-animal to, in the ordinary sense and in the case of limited numbers, supra-mundane. And it appears to be beyond dispute that the majority, if not the first, is a long way from the second." C.H. Douglas, *The Development of World Dominion* (Sydney: Tidal Publications, 1969), 76.

The Root Motive of Human Nature

With respect to the philosophical debate concerning the nature of human motivation, Douglas held that the root or basic motive which actuates human behaviour is that of self-interest:

> **It seems to me that it ought to be evident to anyone of ordinary common sense that the root motive of human nature and the mainspring of human advancement is profit. We never do anything sensible, unless it will be of advantage to us in some sense....[42]**

If this is true, then it follows that any social, economic, or political ideology which ignores this reality is doomed to failure:

> **[A] centralised system of totalitarianism requires, even if it could be made to work, a completely selfless integrity which is not only unknown, but is not Christian. "— thy neighbour as thyself", presumably means what it says.[43]**

Self-interest is not to be identified with selfishness, however (since the pursuit of self-interest need not involve disregarding the rights or legitimate interests of others), nor should Douglas be interpreted as claiming that self-interest is the *only* motive which human nature can admit. On more than one occasion, he affirmed his belief in the existence of genuinely altruistic acts: "Acts of generosity without ulterior motive between individuals are common – between nations or businesses as such, are unknown."[44]

On this particular question, cf. also, John Finlay, *Social Credit the English Origins* (Montreal and London: McGill-Queen's University Press, 1972), 226. According to Finlay, Douglas' meaning in professing disbelief in the dogma was obscured by an unintentional misuse of words: "When Douglas used the term 'original sin,' he was not using it correctly and should have stuck to the alternative which he sometimes used, 'puritanism'."

[42] C.H. Douglas, *Warning Democracy*, 3rd ed. (London: Stanley Nott, 1935), 125.

[43] C.H. Douglas, *The Big Idea* (Bullsbrook, Australia: Veritas Publishing Company, 1983), 66.

[44] C.H. Douglas, *Warning Democracy*, 3rd ed. (London: Stanley Nott, 1935), 75. Cf. C.H. Douglas, *Social Credit*, rev. ed. (New York: Gordon Press, 1973), 171: "Now, we never get mass action out of altruism. Altruism is an occasional characteristic of individuals, never of mobs."

The Social Credit View of the Purpose of Human Life

With respect to the question of what it is which constitutes the ultimate end of human life, Douglas appeared to defend the view that this ultimate purpose could not be known on the basis of natural reason.[45] While remaining within this purely natural perspective, he was nevertheless confident that he could eliminate one possible candidate, 'work as an end in itself':

> I propose to bring as forcibly as possible to your attention that it is not the prime object of existence to find employment. I have no intention of being dogmatic as to what *is* the prime object of existence, but I am entirely confident that it is not comprised in the endless pursuit of turning this originally very beautiful world into slag-heaps, blast-furnaces, guns, and battleships.[46]

Self-Development

Beyond providing us with this indication of what the ultimate end of human life is *not*, our purely natural experience does allow us to obtain a more positive insight regarding the ultimate end of man, namely, that it can only be sought through self-development:

> [T]he end of man, while unknown, is something towards which most rapid progress is made by the free expansion of individuality....[47]

---

[45] Cf. C.H. Douglas, *Warning Democracy*, 3rd ed. (London: Stanley Nott, 1935), 38: "the end of man, while unknown, ..." According to the Christian revelation, the ultimate end of man is the beatific vision, i.e., the eternal vision of God face to face. This is not something which could be discerned on the basis of natural reason and/or experience, and it is, therefore, rightly described as 'unknown' from this point of view. Even so, one must always allow for the possibility that through a *bona fide* religious faith, i.e., through *supernatural* cognition, the human mind could come to know things that are naturally inaccessible.

[46] C.H. Douglas, *Security Institutional and Personal* (Liverpool: K.R.P. Publications Ltd., 1945), 2.

[47] C.H. Douglas, *Warning Democracy*, 3rd ed. (London: Stanley Nott, 1935), 38.

As human individuals develop their capacities, they acquire both superior self-knowledge and superior knowledge of the authentic nature of the universe in which they live. In a very practical sense it is true that knowledge is power and, with an increase in this power, human beings become better placed to discern and to thereby attain to the ultimate end of human existence:

> **In regard to the objective of policy, as applied to human affairs, I can say nothing to you which has not been better said by the great teachers of humanity, One of whom said, "I came that you might have *life* and have it more abundantly." ... In other words, the aim of the *human individual* is ultimately a totalitarian aim, a statement which, if it is correct – that is to say, if it is true that our best interests are served by our ultimately taking a general and effective interest in everything – is, in itself, the negation of the idea of the totalitarian state.[48]**

Indeed, the urge to actualize one's potential as a rational and free being is one of the primary ways that the root motive of human nature, i.e., self-interest, expresses itself. The drive to self-development may therefore be thought of as the proximate end of human nature; it lays the basis for the type of transcendence which the ultimate end would, quite fittingly, appear to require.

The fulfillment of this desire for self-actualization is nevertheless dependent on the fulfillment of a more basic tendency which human beings share with all other living things: the drive to self-preservation. The latter is the first law of human nature and indeed of every living being:

> **[S]elf-preservation is the first law of Nature. Man does not live by bread alone, but he does not live very long without a reasonable amount of food, clothes and shelter.[49]**

---

[48] C.H. Douglas, *The Tragedy of Human Effort* (Vancouver: The Institute of Economic Democracy, 1978), 4.

[49] C.H. Douglas, *These Present Discontents and The Labour Party and Social Credit* (London: Cecil Palmer, 1922), 7.

It is only after the conditions of self-preservation have been fulfilled that human beings are able to distinguish themselves in practice from all other living things by finding "an outlet for the creative spirit."[50] The *spiritual* need for self-expression is the engine which drives individual human development.

To the degree that humans do develop successfully, it is important to re-emphasize that the inequality which characterizes them *ab initio* is not obliterated by their flourishing; on the contrary, under the influence of continual development it tends to become ever more pronounced:

At the root of the growing danger of Government and other embodiments of execution is the idea that human beings are all alike. So far from this being the case, I believe that as human beings develop they become increasingly different.[51]

How is Self-Development Attained?

Restricting ourselves to the natural plane of existence, the fulfillment of human nature requires that the individual be able to mould his environment in keeping with the laws of objective reality (instead of being moulded by force by the power of his environment). Upon the fulfillment of this condition, an individual's environment can acquire the characteristics necessary for his own unique selfhood to flourish with the greatest ease.

The question: 'Is the individual subordinated to the environment or is the environment subordinated to the individual?' is therefore of primary importance where self-development is concerned. The subordination of the individual to the environment tends to thwart the natural developmental

---

[50] Ibid., 7.

[51] C.H. Douglas, *Security Institutional and Personal* (Liverpool: K.R.P. Publications Ltd., 1945), 8. That is, as human beings develop, their personalities and indeed their very being undergo a process of refined differentiation.

Cf. C.H. Douglas, *Major C.H. Douglas Speaks* (Sydney: Douglas Social Credit Association, 1933), 69: "as the human personality develops, it becomes more individualised and specialised in its outlook, and less and less amenable to one universalised set of conditions."

tendencies of the individual, whereas the subordination of the environment to the individual allows for the easy release of his inner potential. As a direct consequence of this law of maturation, frustration and achievement can be taken as alternative signposts on the path of self-development:

Nothing is so destructive as continual frustration (that is one of the worst features of Government Departments) and nothing develops a man like achievement.[52]

Since there are, at least potentially, as many different environments as people, it should be possible to place each individual in a position to survive and flourish as the fittest with respect to the particular environment which happens to best suit his individual nature; i.e., with suitable changes in the social, political, and economic structures, there could be enough privilege for everyone to enjoy.

In order to achieve this subordination of the environment to the individual in lieu of the individual's subordination to the environment, *it is necessary for the individual to possess as much genuine freedom with respect to his associations as possible*; this implies a wide range of options and the acceptance of personal responsibility for the choices made. Freedom in both its negative (freedom from interference) and positive forms (freedom for some purpose) leaves room for the exercise of personal initiative and: "it is out of personal initiative that all progress of any description must come."[53]

Of course, it is simultaneously true that not all choices are necessarily of equal worth. Some facilitate the authentic self-development of the human individual, while others stifle that self-development. It is a primary concern of Social Credit that individuals take personal responsibility for their decisions. The assumption of personal responsibility is crucial, because it enables the only type of progress which ultimately matters, i.e., *moral* progress:

---

[52] C.H. Douglas, *The Big Idea* (Bullsbrook, Australia: Veritas Publishing Company, 1983), 67-68.

[53] C.H. Douglas, *The Control and Distribution of Production* (London: Cecil Palmer, 1922), 119. Cf. C.H. Douglas, *Credit Power and Democracy* (Melbourne: The Social Credit Press, 1933) 6: *"power to make decisions is freedom for the individual, ..."*

There is only one sound basis for co-operative society, and that is individual and personal responsibility.[54]

A civilization is technically advanced to the extent that it has made progress towards the control of its environment with the least amount of exertion necessary on the part of the individual to maintain that control. It is only morally advanced, however, to the extent that it employs this power to further good or sound objectives.

Indeed, the importance of individual responsibility is so great (given its nexus with moral progress) that Douglas insisted that we must start holding people responsible for things that are done under the orders of others. "I was just following orders" must cease to be an acceptable excuse:

If I take a pistol and shoot someone in this room, I am culpable, and have committed a moral crime, and one against the law. But if a war were to break out, and I were to take a machine gun and kill fifty people, it would be a very fine thing, and I perhaps get the V.C.

There is an assumption that responsibility can be taken from a man for his own actions, and put on an organisation, and one of the features of this new Civilisation [which Social Credit wishes to bring about – OH] is that with this individual security must come essential individual responsibility. That is, a thing which is a bad thing, when done under somebody else's orders, is not relieving one of the responsibility for that action.[55]

Provided that personal responsibility can and is being assumed, Douglas also made it clear that no one should have the right, *within the functional limitations of an association*, to interfere with the personal choices of others:

We have to discard the idea that every child is born into the world to mind someone else's business, and substitute the fact that he is

---

[54] C.H. Douglas, *The Big Idea* (Bullsbrook, Australia: Veritas Publishing Company, 1983), 64.

[55] C.H. Douglas, *Major C.H. Douglas Speaks* (Sydney: Douglas Social Credit Association, 1933), 85-86.

responsible for minding his own. That he should help, not meddle.[56]

Individual Happiness and the Value of Human Life.

Finally, while the human person pursues his ultimate end through the various opportunities for self-development, Douglas was keen to point out that we must not lose sight of the fact that the happiness of the individual is at least as important a concern as his ontological value. In other words, man's final destination should not make us insensitive to the quality of his journey:

> It is an unfortunate defect in our attitude towards human affairs that we place an inordinate value upon human life, but a trivial value upon human happiness. You may subject an employee or a member of your family to persistent mental and physical cruelty in the form of bad working conditions, unjust treatment, and a myriad of other minor and major inhumanities, and within very wide limits (and in particular if you do not exceed the conditions which are accepted as normal) it is unlikely that you will receive much criticism. You may lend a widow £20 and make her life a misery by the recovery of interest at 75 per cent per annum, and unless, as is most improbable, she herself takes the matter into court, nothing will be heard of it. But if the widow's son, goaded by his mother's misery, in a fit of uncontrollable rage waylays the money-lender with a coal hammer, and removes that gentleman to other spheres of activity, the son will, in all probability, be hanged, after the whole tremendous machinery of the law has automatically been set in motion for his apprehension and destruction, and the mother will be rendered still more miserable.[57]

---

[56] C.H. Douglas, *The Big Idea* (Bullsbrook, Australia: Veritas Publishing Company, 1983), 58-59.

Cf. Ibid., 70: "And the root of the matter is – mind your own business, and allow no man to make a business of minding you. Listen, in reason, to what advice seems to be backed by proper experience and ability, and pay no attention to windy idealism. And then – mind your own business. It is in sore need of your attention."

[57] C.H. Douglas, *Warning Democracy*, 3rd ed. (London: Stanley Nott, 1935), 187-188.

Chapter Three: Douglas' Philosophy of Action

Like many thinkers before him, Douglas recognized that all of the actions of rational and free human beings, whether they assume a purely individual or collective form, possess an intelligible structure. Beyond the scope of any previous contribution, however, it was one of Douglas' great merits to clearly point out that there is, within the domain of human action, a critical distinction that can and must be drawn between policy and administration.

The Definition of Policy

For Douglas, the term 'policy', whether it be applied within the context of an individual or a group, refers to deliberate action that is taken with some particular end in view and in virtue of some principle of 'what-ought-to-be'. Note that it is not just the end which is important when it comes to grasping the nature of 'policy', but the fact that the end is being *actively* pursued. These two elements combined make policy a sort of living force with which we must contend and which may even be imposed upon us. An end toward which no concrete action has been taken is not yet a policy; it is merely a possible policy-objective:

> **There is a meaning of objective, a strong sense of objective, in the word "policy". ... It is actually, if you like, governmental action, but it is action taken towards a recognised and conscious objective, and it is in that sense that we use the word "policy"; it is a little more, but it comprehends and comprises the word objective.**[58]

In the words of the Australian Social Crediter, Eric Butler, the Social Credit definition of policy might be encapsulated comprehensively as: "the purpose to which power is directed."[59] It is the particular objective which we have chosen to make operative in our actions in accordance with some

---

[58] C.H. Douglas, *The Policy of a Philosophy* (Vancouver: The Institute of Economic Democracy, 1977), 1-2.

[59] Eric Butler, *Social Dynamics* (Fitzroy, Australia: W. & J. Barr Pty. Ltd., date unknown), 3. An alternative formulation of the same definition would be 'power directed to a purpose'.

principle, rule, or norm of behaviour.

The Definition of Administration

In contrast to policy, we can also distinguish the *means* or *methods* which might be employed by an individual or group in the pursuit of a policy-objective. Chief amongst these means are the various forms of organization that may be adopted by a human association. These forms of organization are instances of 'administration'. In general, administration may be defined as "a concerted attempt at co-operation for the attainment of a given policy."[60]

The Relation of Policy and Administration to 'Philosophy'

Now all policies, without exception, are based on or presuppose some 'philosophy' or conception of reality (the same could be said, *mutatis mutandis*, of the various models of administration). What men believe (i.e., hold as true) governs what they do:

> If there is one thing which seems to me beyond dispute, it is that you cannot have a policy (here I use the word again in the way in which I have defined it), the policy of a country, policy of a race, or of a nation, without having a philosophy behind it. You cannot have a bridge without a model and drawing behind it, or without having had a desire to have a bridge. ... I am absolutely convinced myself that there must be somewhere behind the policy a philosophy, or you cannot have a policy.[61]

---

[60] C.H. Douglas, *Major C.H. Douglas Speaks* (Sydney: Douglas Social Credit Association, 1933), 78.

[61] C.H. Douglas, *The Policy of a Philosophy* (Vancouver: The Institute of Economic Democracy, 1977), 4. Cf. C.H. Douglas, *The Big Idea* (Bullsbrook, Australia: Veritas Publishing Company, 1983), 3: "Where it is possible to identify a continuous organisation, it is safe to postulate a continuous policy, and as every policy besides having a philosophy, has an appropriate mechanism, or form of organisation, it is also safe to conclude that similar mechanisms have similar policies and philosophies, ..." Cf. also: C.H. Douglas, *"Whose Service is Perfect Freedom"* (Bullsbrook, Western Australia: 1983), 4: "every policy has a philosophy, very often widely different from that which its supporters claim for it ..."

The fact that there are different policies and also different forms of administration that are grounded in different 'philosophies', and the fact that these different 'philosophies' represent, to one extent or another, mutually exclusive conceptions of reality, mean that human beings are forced to choose which policies and forms of administration they will adopt and which they will reject. A choice amongst incompatible policies and forms of administration is possible because policy and administration are operative in the sphere of what Douglas refers to as 'conventional' as opposed to 'natural' laws:

> [W]e are familiar with two kinds of laws. There is natural law of the nature of the conditions which compel a stone to fall when it is dropped from a height, and which, if it falls, let us say, in a vacuum, always falls at the same rate of acceleration under the compulsion of gravity. That is a natural law, and, so far as we know, those laws are compelling laws. We cannot change the laws of that description, and all we can do is adjust ourselves to those laws.
>
> But there is also a second type of law, a law which is what we may call conventional law. Of course, our legal laws – the laws of our Government – are conventional laws. We have agreed to rule ourselves by those conventions. On a smaller scale, of course, we have the same sort of thing in connection with playing a game.
>
> We agree that, in a game we call cricket, if the ball is struck by the batsman and is caught by a fielder before it touches the ground the batsman is out. We are not obliged to have conventions of that sort. We could change them if we found that we could improve cricket by some other convention. ....
>
> Now, the first requisite in any understanding of this position on the basis of what I have just been saying is to recognise that what we refer to as conventional laws are matters of policy. You do not make a conventional law without having some sort of an idea in your mind as to what it is you are trying to do – what end you are endeavouring to serve.
>
> If you make a law that all motor-cars shall drive on the left-hand side of the road, you have in your mind that in that way you will avoid collisions, and you have a policy in your mind in making such a law that you want to avoid collisions of motor-cars.[62]

---

[62] C.H. Douglas, *The Use of Money* (Liverpool: K.R.P. Publications Ltd., 1934), 3-4.

Even though policies rely on conventional laws or rules, it is not the case that all policies are of equal worth and this is connected with the fact that not all of their underlying 'philosophies' are of equal value as conceptions of reality. Some 'philosophies' are true or at least closer to the truth than others, while other 'philosophies' are false. If the particular 'philosophy' upon which a policy is based is false, the policy will prove to be a failure (it will not deliver the proper results) and, depending on the case, may even be fatal. Perhaps the objectives set out by the policy are at odds with the objective nature of reality (i.e., perhaps one is trying to achieve some end in defiance of reality), or perhaps the end is sound but the particular administrative means prescribed by the underlying 'philosophy' are not the best available. The relationship existing between a disastrous policy and a false 'philosophy' was once explained by Eric Butler in the following terms:

If a person crossing a street believes that the street is free of all traffic, then he proceeds to cross confident that he may do so safely. His policy is based upon the situation *as he sees it*. But should his concept of the situation be faulty, and he has not seen a fast-moving car, then his policy will bring him into violent conflict with reality *as it is*.[63]

Good or correct policies, i.e., policies that are truly satisfactory, must be rooted in a realistic 'philosophy', i.e., one which adequately reflects reality. Bad or incorrect policies are those which deliver unsatisfactory results, and they are rooted in unrealistic 'philosophies', i.e., conceptions which do not adequately reflect reality. Similarly, good or correct means or forms of administration are also grounded in a true 'philosophy', whereas bad or incorrect means or forms of administration stem from a false 'philosophy'.

If a particular 'philosophy' turns out to be a correct conception of reality with respect to ends, means, and their proper interrelation, action based on it will be able to achieve astonishing results:

To my mind the whole thing depends upon this question of reality. If you are working in accordance with something which is real (and when I say real, I mean something which is in the nature of the uni-

---

[63] Eric Butler, *Social Dynamics* (Fitzroy, Australia: W. & J. Barr Pty. Ltd., date unknown), 4.

verse, in the same way as the law of gravity is in the nature of the universe), you will get results which cannot be got even if you are working along proper lines for something which is unreal.[64]

Action based on sounder philosophies therefore make for better policies and better forms of administration.[65]

Determining which policies are correct and which of the available means are most appropriate is therefore a matter of determining which 'philosophies' or propositional pictures of reality are true and which are false. But before one can decide which 'philosophies' *ought* to be held on account of their truth-value, and then which 'policies' and 'means' *ought* to be adopted, one must acquire a correct notion of the nature of the 'ought'.

---

[64] C.H. Douglas, *The Policy of a Philosophy* (Vancouver: The Institute of Economic Democracy, 1977), 15. This particular excerpt continues as follows:

"I believe the whole philosophy of the modern world is essentially unreal. Never before have we been going through such an orgy of calculated delusions raised upon a conception, which is consciously vicious, of what is important in the world; and up to a certain point it succeeds.

There is a curious potency in a correct technique, applied to an essential proposition or objective, which makes it succeed.

Good will always be vanquished by evil, so long as evil understands its tools better than good; but if good can only be taught to use its tools correctly, the good will vanquish evil."

[65] Cf. C.H. Douglas, *The Policy of a Philosophy* (Vancouver: The Institute of Economic Democracy, 1977), 11: "Our new philosophy will change the run of the universe at once. It will enable you to have a new conception ... you will, in an incredibly short time, become the most formidable force that the world holds, because you will have, in my opinion, the sounder philosophy, and you would have, in that philosophy, a better policy."

The Nature of the Ought

If we claim that a policy is correct, we are in fact affirming that it *ought* to be selected. If, on the other hand, we assert that a policy is incorrect we are affirming that it *ought* not to be selected. Contrary to the impression which some may derive from a reading of primary source material, it is not true to claim that Douglas rejected 'the ought' as meaningless; his writings frequently present claims involving 'oughts' and 'shoulds.' Douglas acknowledged that there are indeed certain actions which are objectively preferable to others. At the same time, he recognized that 'ought-thinking' can be exceedingly dangerous if it is grounded in a false 'philosophy': it often leads to the zealous and stubborn adherence to policies which prove themselves in practice to be disastrous. It is for this reason that Douglas advocated what might be termed the *realistic* as opposed to the *idealistic* ought.[66]

In response to the question: 'what should we do?', the realistic ought stipulates that, in whatever field of endeavour, we should always conform ourselves (our actions) with the objective nature of reality (of how things actually are) in order to achieve the best possible outcome of which reality can admit. Eric Butler referred to this course of action as 'releasing reality'. The idealistic ought, by contrast, claims that we should always act in order to conform reality with our ideas about how things ought to be. Whenever we act we are therefore always faced with this choice between 'what ought to be' according to the objective nature of reality and 'what ought to be' according to man's mind and will – independently of, or in defiance of, that reality.

---

[66] While these specific terms were not used by Douglas to describe the corresponding phenomena, the underlying distinction is to be found in his writings. For example, in his work *The Brief for the Prosecution*, Douglas implicitly contrasted deductive policies which appeal to ideals divorced from reality, with inductive policies, which are grounded on what is given in experience: "Faced with policies of a deductive character, based, not so much on experience as on ideals, (using the word in its popular, rather than true sense), the 'practical' man has a strong tendency to allow himself to be deprived of the tools of his own method." C.H. Douglas, *The Brief for the Prosecution* (Liverpool: K.R.P. Publications Ltd., 1945), 1. In other words, all policies invoke or presuppose the claim that some course of action *ought* to be, but this claim can be buttressed either by what has proven itself to work best in experience (the realistic ought), or else by a vision of what and how things ought to be independently of experience (the idealistic ought), a vision which, for one reason or another, is appealing to the individual or group.

The two approaches have two entirely different points of departure or frames of reference and they also seek to yield two entirely different types of results. The realistic ought discounts all self-contained theories about what or how things ought to be and starts from the reality of what is (the normative is grounded in the descriptive); it claims that the purpose of consciously directed action is not to change reality into something else, but rather *to release the innate potential of reality* so that the best things that actually can be will in fact be.[67] That which works best is viewed as normative. When one considers that the achievement of optimal functioning is dependent, in the first place, on how things are designed or on their essences, the realistic ought amounts to a recognition that things work best when they are empowered to operate in accordance with their own deepest nature and that the policies or actions that we should select are those which are most likely to be *successful* amongst the available alternatives.[68] The idealistic ought, on the other hand, starts from a self-contained theory of how things should be (the normative is grounded in the ideal) and claims that the purpose of consciously directed action is to transform or change reality so that it will conform to that abstract vision. It is, in fact, a vain attempt to change reality into something which it cannot,

---

[67] It might be objected that attempting to ground the normative in the descriptive is bound to commit the naturalistic fallacy, or the mistake of attempting to deduce normative conclusions from contingent facts. While it is true that any argument trying to derive an 'ought' by appealing to contingent facts about nature is necessarily invalid, it is also true that not all facts about nature are contingent. Necessary essences and essential relations can be embodied in concretely existing things. Grounding normative conclusions on these necessities as they appear in concretely existing things can provide a sufficient justification for normative judgements of the realistic persuasion.

[68] In this, there can be no room for a blind dogmatism of any type; as soon as it becomes evident that some other course of action outside of an established theory is actually the one which works best in obtaining the intended results, it should, *ceteris paribus*, be adopted and the theory revised. Similarly, if, in a certain field of endeavour, one is entirely unsure as to which course of action will work best, then one should test the available options and proceed by a process of modification and elimination. If x does not work best under conditions a, b, and c, then either x is somehow a wrong approach in itself or it should be engaged in under different conditions such as d, e, and f, etc. If the particular ought-principle passes the test (i.e., has not been falsified) by always producing the intended results with better degrees of efficacy and efficiency in comparison with other alternatives, then it is safe to conclude that it is probably the course of action which will work best in that particular situation.

either in principle or as a matter of fact, become.[69] It is in this sense that the ideal (i.e., what the human mind conjures up on its own as 'what ought to be' in violation of the true nature of things) is the enemy of the real.

In dealing with various prescriptions for the economic malaise which afflicted Europe after the First World War, Douglas noted that many of these remedial proposals were based on the idealistic ought, and he contrasted this type of approach with its realistic alternative:

> All these schemes are *deductive* in character; they start with a theory of a different sort of society to the one we know, and assume that the problem is to change the world into that form. In consequence, all the solutions demand centralisation of administration; they involve a machinery by which individuals can be forced to do something – work, fight, etc.; the machine must be stronger than the man. ...
>
> It may be observed, however, that in the world in which things are actually done, not talked about, where bridges are built, engines are made, armies fight, we do not work that way. We do not sit down in London and say the Forth Bridge ought to be 500 yards long and 50 ft. high, and then make such a bridge and narrow down the Firth of Forth by about 75 per cent. and cut off the masts of every steamer 45 ft. above sea-level in order to make them pass under it. We measure the Firth, observe the ships, and make our structure fit our facts. Successful generals do not say "The proper place to fight the battle is at X, I am not interested in what the other fellow is doing, I shall move all my own troops there."[70]

In order to make this distinction between the realistic and idealistic ought even clearer, it will be useful to consider an additional, concrete example. Let us assume that a group of men wish to build an aeroplane that will safely and efficiently transport passengers from one continent to another. Given this objective they can either a) build the plane in

---

[69] The idealistic ought belongs, therefore, either to the realm of the intrinsically or the momentarily impossible; i.e., it is a futile attempt to subordinate reality to an abstraction. Since it is at odds with the nature of things, action based on it is doomed to fail, either in the short or long-term.

[70] C.H. Douglas, *The Control and Distribution of Production* (London: Cecil Palmer, 1922), 64-65.

accordance with the principles of aerodynamics as they are and show themselves to be in experience, independently of anyone's thinking or perception, or else b) build the plane in accordance with what they think the principles of aerodynamics *ought to be* according to some self-contained theory which appeals to their vanity, serves their need for intellectual security, facilitates certain political or commercial goals, or reflects some pragmatic set of preferences, etc. Only in the first case will the proper materials be selected and brought into the correct association with each other so that the goal of safely and efficiently transporting passengers can be achieved. Since it is the successful path, it is what the men ought to do, but notice that its success is very much dependent on a realistic approach to the task at hand, i.e., acting in keeping with how things really are and not as we would have them.

If one likes, the truth of the matter could be expressed in this way: what we *ought* to do is to adopt the realistic ought in all circumstances since it is, of the two orientations, the only one that can actually deliver satisfactory results. Accordingly, Douglas never believed that any problem should be tackled with the mindset of 'this is how I think things ought to work', but rather with the desire of wanting to discover how things actually do work when they are empowered to act in accordance with their own natures.[71]

There is one further distinction, however, within the realm of the realistic ought which must be clearly drawn. While the realistic ought always designates that course of action which works best, some of these courses of action may depend on circumstances and conditions which are *beyond the control of the individual*. There is, in other words, what we might term 'the impracticable realistic ought', in comparison with 'the practicable realistic ought.' Individuals must not fall into the trap of thinking that all realistic oughts, or the policies which would in fact work best, can be immediately or easily implemented and that any failure to do that which works best

---

[71] The attentive reader will note that the idealistic ought is present in all worldviews that are contaminated with kabbalistic thinking. In contrast to theosophy, various 'new age' philosophies, the advice given in 'The Secret', etc., which all claim that the way to get satisfactory results is to make the universe bend itself to your desires by *believing* in whatever you want to exist as already real, Douglas' realistic ought proclaims that truly satisfactory results can only come from respecting reality, discovering its objective facts and laws, and then applying these in order to obtain what is truly beneficial *within the nature of things*. The path to genuine and lasting success lies in conforming one's mind and will to reality, and not in attempting, regardless of any apparent successes, to conform reality to one's mind and will.

must therefore be the responsibility of the individual in question. To believe that one ought to undertake actions which are impracticable simply because they also happen to fall into the category of the realistic ought is to reintroduce the mindset of the idealistic ought: 'since x represents the realistic ought it ought also (according to my thinking or wishes) to be practicable and in my power to effect.' While neither underestimating nor overestimating the scope of limitation, individuals *ought* to humbly accept whatever limitations are inherent in the nature of things and not try to pursue a realistic ought in an idealistic way. The consequences of trying to impose a realistic ought in the face of one's natural limitations can only lead to distress and make one even less effective in accomplishing the sort of realistic goals that would otherwise be attainable. On this particular matter, Douglas gave the following piece of advice:

> **[W]hat you can do [about anything - OH] is just as much inherent in the nature of things as the trouble about the monetary system. The key to an undertaking of this slightly subtle matter is that the question of works as opposed to faith depends obviously on ability. Nobody can be held responsible for something they don't understand or cannot do. I want you to keep that in mind.[72]**

The Canon

In line with the realistic conception of the ought, determining which types of actions are correct and which are incorrect, and which of the constituent policies and means are correct and which are incorrect, requires that we measure them against some objective standard. Douglas recognized, like many Western thinkers before him, that reality is governed by laws (i.e., things either are or behave in certain set ways under defined conditions). These laws are independent of human thinking, perception, or preference.[73] Some of them are philosophical or mathematical in nature (i.e., they are *a priori* laws), while others are scientific or historical, etc. (i.e., they are empirical or *a posteriori* laws). In their totality, Douglas referred to these laws as constituting what he termed a 'Canon':

---

[72] C.H. Douglas, *The Approach to Reality* (London: K.R.P. Publications Ltd., 1936), 12.

[73] Cf. C.H. Douglas, *Realistic Constitutionalism* (London: K.R.P. Publications Ltd., 1947), 3: "the rules of the Universe transcend human thinking, and cannot, in the ordinary sense of the words, be altered, and therefore must be ascertained and obeyed."

[T]here is running through the nature of the Universe something that we may call a "canon". It is the thing which is referred to in the Gospel of St. John as the "Logos," the "Word" (Logos: "The Word" or "Reason"). [St. John 1:1, "The Word (Logos) was with God, and the Word was God." ...] It has an infinite variety of names. The engineer and the artist refer to it when they say that they have got something "right". Other people mean the same thing when they talk about absolute truth, or reality. By whatever name you wish to refer to this idea, it does not matter very much; we all instinctively recognise its existence whether we meet it in something like architectural pro-portions as, say, the cenotaph, or even in the grim lines of a battle-ship.[74]

The Canon is of supreme importance when it comes to determining the course of human actions, whether they be individual or collective in nature, because these actions can only produce their intended results if they are in conformity with the Canon (i.e., if they are in conformity with the laws governing reality). A consistent pattern of successful action requires, therefore, that the relevant laws of the Canon be properly under-stood and that they be effectively applied through suitable mechanisms. It requires the proper integration of the *correct* ends with the *correct* means:

Genuine success only accompanies a consistent attempt to discover and to conform to this canon in no matter what sphere our activities may lie.[75]

In other words, our faculty of free will does not give us the power to make or alter the laws of the universe in order to suit ourselves.

[74] C.H. Douglas, *Major C.H. Douglas Speaks* (Sydney: Douglas Social Credit Association, 1933), 52-53. In introducing this particular paragraph, Douglas wrote: "... it is my own belief, and I might almost say that it is almost my only religion, [please note the two qualifiers – OH] that there is ... a 'canon'". There are many points of commonality between Douglas' notions of the 'canon', and how we should behave in relation to it, and the teachings of Zoroastrianism concerning 'asha' (the truth of the universe's right order), and our responsibility to live in accordance with this body of truth by practising good thoughts, words, and deeds.

[75] Ibid., 53. On this same page (53), Douglas went on to note that one must be very careful in distinguishing the Canon from the manifestations of the Canon in specific times and places: "Because the canon is a spiritual thing, the forms embodying it are of infinite variety, and, not only that, change from time to time, and a slavish adherence to the form is a certain method by which to miss the canon."

Acting in ways which, either at the level of objectives (i.e., policy) or those of methods (i.e., administration, etc.), are at odds with this Canon, will invariably fail to produce the intended results. This will lead to dissatisfaction, and is indeed likely to produce a series of unfortunate states of affairs which are directly opposed to those results which the agents in question presumably desire.[76] One of the central claims of the Social Credit worldview is that much, if not the vast majority of both of the 'positive' and 'negative' forms of dissatisfaction which people experience with their economic, political, and cultural associations, is "the direct result of endeavouring to carry on the business of the world in accordance with a defective conception or idea."[77]

To the extent that the actions of individuals and groups deviate unintentionally from the Canon, and, in consequence, yield undesirable results, the misdirection of their activity is due, at least proximately, to their holding false ideas about reality which they are relying on in order to orient their interactions with that reality. We often speak of things as if they were different from what they really are and are often supported in our disinclination to bring our views into conformity with reality by vested interests who appear to gain in direct proportion to the degree to which these false beliefs are widely disseminated:

---

[76] It is important to re-emphasize that it is not enough to have adopted a right policy or a sound policy to achieve success; one must also employ the best available means for that particular policy: "a comprehension of a sound policy is by no means an identity with a comprehension of the means by which it may be achieved.

The first may be emotional or intuitional; but the second must be technical." C.H. Douglas, *The Brief for the Prosecution* (Liverpool: K.R.P. Publications Ltd., 1945), 64.

[77] C.H. Douglas, *Major C.H. Douglas Speaks* (Sydney: Douglas Social Credit Association, 1933), 52. By 'positive' dissatisfaction, I am referring to the *presence* of some negative result, whereas, by 'negative' dissatisfaction, I am referring to the *absence* of a due good.

Just as there is a 'Canon', there is also an 'anti-Canon', or, better yet, a plurality of anti-Canons that tend to have certain basic (and false) premises in common. Action which is based on a false conception of the facts of the world and/or on false values/principles leads to the incarnation of evil or dysfunction on the practical plane. The denial of the existence of spiritual or metaphysical values as such, as is found in metaphysical materialism, for example, reveals itself as false by the negative metaphysical consequences which materialism in the narrower sense (i.e., consumerism) engenders in a society that is built upon such a doctrine. Man cannot and indeed does not live (i.e., fully flourish) by bread (i.e., the attainment of material well-being) alone.

Running through all history like the thread of Ariadne, it is possible to trace a continuous policy which I can only describe as a divorce between things themselves and the description of them. A well-known instance of this, of course, is the glamour of war. War, at any rate modern war, is a dirty, beastly, inhumane, insane undertaking, proving nothing, adding nothing to the content of human values, and incidentally definitely dysgenic, having a strong tendency to kill off the best of the stock, and to leave the weakling to carry on the race. Not only that, but the conditions which accompany a war give play to intrigue, corruption, tyranny, and wire-pulling under cover of the suppression of publicity and the necessity for centralised control which are imposed by the exigencies of the struggle. Yet no war was ever carried on without a definite organisation to represent it as being in some way magnificent, glorious, and ennobling.

This antithesis is a commonplace, and forms the basis of the misguided activities of pacifists unable to recognise that without a rectification of the causes of war, the suppression of war is as likely to be productive of good results as is plunging a sufferer from measles into cold water for the purpose of driving in the spots.

We are beginning to recognise, however, that this constant tendency to present a false picture of what is actually going on in the world extends all through our civilisation.[78]

Of course, the very fact that vested interests can achieve selfish gains by distorting people's conceptions of reality is an indication that deviations from the Canon are not always unintentional or due to a lack of sufficient information or intelligence. Sometimes people purposely rebel against the laws of the universe (i.e., God's laws) because they interfere with some sort of subjective satisfaction which they wish to achieve for themselves at the expense of reality. They announce to themselves and to others that they don't like such and such a law and that things ought not to be the way they are. What they are in fact doing is deliberately basing their actions on the idealistic ought in defiance of reality. This sort of deviation from the Canon is due to an immoral attitude, a sort of metaphysical pride. Such people have an expectation that reality should be subject to their will in its very constitution, as if they were gods.

---

[78] Ibid., 48.

Attempts at rebellion are ultimately futile as every act of disobedience where the Canon is concerned merely succeeds in demonstrating the truth of the laws which govern the universe. As G.K. Chesterton used to say, jumping off of a cliff does not break the law of gravity, it only confirms its truth, just as the pitiful political, economic, cultural, and environmental conditions in which our world presently finds itself also reveal the truth inherent in the divine design.

In the case of unintentional deviations from the Canon, the only thing that can put an end to the pathetic misdirection of so much effort is a knowledge of truth:

At this very period in which we live, it is probable that one of the fundamental struggles which is taking place, and one on which the future of civilisation depends perhaps more than on any other, is the attempt to obtain an atonement, or as it has been pronounced an at-onement, between reality and the description of it.[79]

As a matter of fact, the body of thought known as Social Credit may be conceived as nothing more nor less than the attempt to discover that part of the Canon which deals with the proper functioning of political, economic, and other types of associations, and to design appropriate mechanisms by means of which the relevant canonical truths may be successful applied to yield satisfactory results. Once laid out in a systematic manner, the truth will sweep away the body of abstractions which presently obscures it in the minds of the otherwise well-meaning, together with the tremendous dissatisfaction which action based on falsehood engenders.[80]

---

[79] Ibid., 48-49.

Cf. also, Ibid., 54: "just as departure from the canon has produced the appalling condition of the world at the present time so the existence of a growing body of people who are aware of the situation, and singly devoted to bringing back UNDERSTANDING into relation with REALITY, constitutes not only the great, but the only certainty that eventually a world system founded UPON LIES will give way to one which is formed upon TRUTH."

[80] Cf. C.H. Douglas, "*Whose Service is Perfect Freedom*" (Bullsbrook, Western Australia: 1983), 13: "it has become clear to me that the difficulties which confront the world's miserable struggles towards sanity, are not in the main intellectual difficulties; they are almost wholly problems of de-hypnotisation, ..."

In the case of intentional deviations from the Canon, these also require a *metanoia* or moral conversion; a task which is nevertheless made easier the more one achieves a fuller knowledge of the truth.[81]

The Criterion of Criteria: Discerning the Content of the Canon and the Truth Generally

Since successful activity is dependent on a knowledge and correct application of the laws composing the Canon, it is critical for human beings to exercise the capacity to discern truth from error. This capacity is itself dependent on many different factors, including intellectual, psychological, experiential, moral, and methodological factors, etc. Some of these elements may be largely beyond human control, while others can be voluntarily brought into alignment by following the prescriptions of the Canon in regard to them. In what follows, we will concern ourselves with the methodological pre-conditions for the discovery of truth.

The Key to the Canon:
the Phenomenological Criterion for the Discernment of Truth

If the end of intellectual inquiry is the attainment of truth, or, in the words of Sir Francis Bacon, "restoring or cultivating a just and legitimate familiarity between the mind, and things",[82] then the proper *methods* must be employed if this end is to be fulfilled in an effective and efficient manner. This question of proper methods involves identifying, *inter alia*, the correct criterion which is to be used in order to *discern* the truth.

There is, in other words, a law governing the way in which truth is to be sought or discovered. This methodological law has yet to be brought to a full *prise de conscience* and many individuals still operate in defiance of it; but it is also certain that none of the steady scientific and technological progress which humanity has made throughout the last few centuries

---

[81] Might it be that a perfect knowledge of a truth *must* result in the compliance of the will in respecting that truth? The ancient Greek philosopher Socrates was of the confirmed opinion that no one does wrong willingly.

[82] As quoted in C.H. Douglas, *The Brief for the Prosecution* (Liverpool: K.R.P. Publications Ltd., 1945), 5.

could have been achieved without at least an implicit recognition of and obedience to that law:

> **All progress in the world, and in some ways the world has un-questionably made progress, has been achieved by recognition of TRUTH, and the reason that so little progress has been made in the solution of social problems is, to my mind, because in this sphere alone truth has been ignored or denied.**[83]

Let us take it as an axiom that, as far as human beings are concerned, one specific form of epistemic truth, i.e., the *knowledge* of propositional truth, consists in the conformity of the human mind with reality. This can be contrasted with logical or propositional truth in and of itself. A proposition is true when the state of affairs which it posits as obtaining actually does obtain in reality. A proposition is known to be true when a person has adequate reasons for *holding* that such a true proposition is in fact true. In both cases, truth consists in a kind of correspondence.

Whenever a person establishes in his mind a propositional picture of the world which he takes to be a true representation of that world he is developing what might be termed, in the broadest possible sense, a theory or, perhaps better put, a theoretical vision of the world. That propositional picture is only true if the actual states of affairs in the world, i.e., the facts, correspond to the states of affairs which the propositional picture posits. But how can anyone ever know or at least have good reasons for believing that a given theoretical vision of the world actually is true, either in whole or in part? How can we know or at least have good reasons for believing in any particular case that a proposition actually does correspond with the state of affairs which it posits and that in affirming such a proposition our minds are indeed in conformity with reality?

Several criteria for discerning truth have been proposed or tacitly relied on throughout the history of civilization. Such standards include things such as custom, tradition, time, feelings, instincts, hunches, majority rule, *consensus gentium*, authority, consistency, coherence, and explanatory pow-

---

[83] C.H. Douglas, *Major C.H. Douglas Speaks* (Sydney: Douglas Social Credit Association, 1933), 47.

er. It is sometimes claimed, for example, that some proposition should be accepted as true because most people believe it to be true, or because it has traditionally been held to be true, or because it coheres well with a certain worldview or theory that is generally accepted as true, etc.

There are, broadly speaking, two factors or variables at play with respect to this question of discerning the truth: theory and facts. The criteria we have looked at so far have one thing in common: they all evaluate the truth-value of theoretical content in terms of other theoretical considerations as opposed to something which lies beyond the realm of theory altogether. In doing so, they all end up subordinating fact to theory. That is, theory becomes more important for determining what we think and hold about the nature of the world than the facts which are or could be given to us in experience. These criteria are all, in fact, applications of the idealistic ought; i.e., they are attempts to determine what we ought to hold as true based on what reality ought to be according to some theoretical set of considerations.

There is one criterion for discerning the truth which distinguishes itself by the fact that it takes the opposite approach. As such, it represents an application of the realistic ought with respect to this particular issue; i.e., it holds that we ought to affirm propositions as true based on what and how reality actually is. At the beginning of the 20th century, Edmund Husserl, the phenomenologist, explicitly directed the attention of the philosophical world to this criterion for the discernment of truth for the first time and so it may justly be referred to as the 'phenomenological criterion'. According to this principle, the supreme standard of truth (within the limits of natural human cognition) is the evidence given to us in conscious experience. In order to find the truth, the world of theory must be routinely subordinated to the world of fact, and the only way of achieving this sub-ordination, as far as natural human reason is concerned, is to make what is given in experience the *principium* (the determining factor) of all that we hold theoretically about the nature of the world. 'Theory' is then put in its proper place as the *principiatum* (the determined factor).

Simply stated, the phenomenological criterion for the discernment of truth (i.e., for the discovery of truth and the evaluation of truth-claims) is that a proposition can be known as true or at least reasonably believed to be true if the proposition corresponds in its content and modality *with what is given in conscious experience*. If a proposition merely fails to correspond because of an absence of relevant facts, it might still be true, although it could not be known or reasonably believed to be such. If, on the other hand, the proposition actually contradicts what is given in experience, then, depending on the nature of the experience and the modality of what is given, the proposition might be regarded either as demonstrably false, probably false, or at least questionable.

The greatest methodological barrier to the acquisition of truth by human beings has been the tendency, whether due to ignorance, laziness, or else psychological, sociological, or political factors, to put theory ahead of the data of experience and to re-interpret the latter in the light of the former. The marked tendency to subordinate the real (i.e., the mind-independent world) to the ideal (i.e., the way in which we conceive of the world) in conducting an investigation of reality is an inversion of the due order and can only be productive of bad consequences.

Instead, if we wish to discover truth we must be ever willing to revise and even discard theory in the light of the facts of experience. Abstractions must be subordinated to reality rather than reality being subordinated to abstractions. Only thus can we put an end to the "divergence between facts, and the presentation of the facts, ..."[84] Only thus do we have any hope of ascertaining the Canon in every field of human endeavour and of applying that knowledge through the design of suitable mechanisms to the ever greater satisfaction of mankind.

While Douglas did not use the term 'phenomenological' to describe the correct criterion for discerning truth, and had, as far as the present writer is aware, no contact with the phenomenological movement, he implicitly recognized it as the correct standard when he once contrasted the anti-phenomenological approach with the phenomenological approach to the discernment of truth as the deductive vs. the inductive 'habit of mind':

> [T]he advance of the world – the progress of the world – depends ultimately upon what I might call a point of view. And the world has been for a considerable time operating, as you might say, within two divergent points of view, one of which is old – as we count age – and one of which has a later origin to which I will refer.
>
> The first of these points of view, or habits of mind, as you might say, is called by those people who deal in the science of logic, the

---

[84] C.H. Douglas, *Major C.H. Douglas Speaks* (Sydney: Douglas Social Credit Association, 1933), 49.

DEDUCTIVE habit of mind, which may be translated as the habit of arguing from the general to the particular. ...

Supposing you had never seen a cow, and the first sight that you had of a cow was on the skyline standing still. You would see a silhouette of a cow, and it would appear to have two legs and someone would say, "That is a cow!" Now, if you had the deductive habit of mind you would immediately form a theory about cows and you would say "That is a cow. All cows are black, all cows have two legs, and all cows stand still." And when somebody pointed out to you in the plains a red animal with white spots moving rapidly you would deny that that could possibly be a cow. No cow could possibly exhibit four legs, have white spots, or move about. You have a fixed theory about cows, and your consequent theory about cows does not fit in with that theory, and, therefore it is not a cow. ....

Now the great defect of the deductive habit of mind is that it is static, that it forms a theory – just as I was suggesting you could form a theory about cows – and in its pure form that theory is eternal. No facts will shift it at all. Anything that does not conform with that theory is not a fact.

This deductive habit of mind persisted long before the Christian era until down to about the middle of the 16th century, when a man arose who became Lord Chancellor of England – Francis Bacon – and he wrote two books, one of which was called "On the Advancement of Learning" and the other was called the "Novum Organum," which no doubt most of you know means "New Method". ... Bacon said: "Further speculation along the lines of these great ancients is fruit-less. What is required is to cultivate the just relationship between the mind and things."

Now that may – if you sort it out of its rather ancient English – seem to you to be a very obvious thing for anybody to say, but it was a completely new idea. It was an absolutely revolutionary method of thinking. It was the birth of the experimental method.

From that time onwards in certain lines of activity, instead of its being possible to set up a theory, and say that theory is a good theory, and is eternal, we have got into the habit of mind in certain spheres of activity of saying any fact is a good fact .... but any theory against which anybody can bring a fact which will not fit into it, is a bad theory and should be discarded. ...

Now, up to the time of and, of course, for some time after the formulation of this theory, which is called the INDUCTIVE method of thinking – the method of arguing from facts to a tentative theory which you discard as soon as it ceases to coincide with the facts, and this is the reverse of the idea of forming a rigid theory and blinding yourself to the fact – up to the time that this new inductive method of thought came into operation, I should like you to observe that from the material point of view the world made no progress whatever. *The method by which people got food, board and clothes, and kept themselves against the storms, and the way they built ships, and the way they progressed – their transportation – and so forth, made for all practical purposes no advance whatever in the centuries, thousands of years, between the birth of Christ and the sixteenth century – none whatever.*

The formulation of a fixed set of ideas is a disregarding of facts. The world was warned against it nineteen hundred years ago, or so, when it was said that the letter killeth, but the spirit maketh alive.[85]

---

[85] C.H. Douglas, "Major Douglas at Dunedin" *The Social Credit Standard*, No. 9 (July-August, 1934), 1-2.

Cf. C.H. Douglas, *Social Credit*, rev. ed. (New York: Gordon Press, 1973), 50:

"But the great danger of placing too much reliance on the deductive method, is that the whole of its conclusions are rendered misleading and dangerous if an essential factor is omitted from the premises."

The empiricism championed by Francis Bacon has led to tremendous material progress because, under its influence, the modern experimental method employs the correct criterion for discerning truth and evaluating truth-claims: the test of what is given in experience. Empiricism errs, however, in assuming that human experience is limited to sense experience, or more broadly, to the experience of blunt contingencies. It seems to me that authentic spiritual progress has, to a very large extent, eluded humanity because the phenomenological criterion has not yet been widely applied to the discernment of truth, either within the sphere of the *a priori* (or necessary states of affairs) or to the sphere of highly intelligible but contingent states of affairs.

Douglas would appear to have been on the same general trajectory of thought when he claimed that engineering methodology can and should be applied to other spheres of being beyond that of the merely material:

Douglas' advocacy of the 'inductive habit of thought' which is, for all intents and purposes, identical with the phenomenological approach towards the discernment of truth means that Douglas, in addition to being a metaphysical and epistemological realist, was a methodological realist:

It is very much better that philosophies should follow facts than that facts should be constrained in accordance with philosophies.[86]

One natural consequence of the consistent and complete adoption of this 'inductive habit of thought' is Douglas' great intellectual openness, an openness which all thinkers should seek to possess:

I do not think that our knowledge of the real nature of the universe in which we live is anything like sufficient to justify ridicule in regard to any theory which has not been very fully investigated.[87]

From a practical point of view, the proof that one's theoretical vision of the world is out of step, whether substantially or partially, with reality, is that action based on such a vision will fail to be optimally functional (within the natural limitations imposed by circumstance):

"In defining the profession of engineering as the application of the forces of nature to the uses of man, the Institution of Civil Engineers no doubt had in mind those forces which at the present time we are accustomed to call physical forces. There is no reason to limit the definition of such forces, and it is becoming increasingly recognised that the province of the engineer, and in particular the scope of engineering method, can with advantage be extended to cover forces of a more metaphysical and psychological character." C.H. Douglas, *The Monopoly of Credit*, 4th ed. (Sudbury: Bloomfield Books, 1979), 153.

In describing the engineering method, Douglas went on to note that: "In attacking an engineering problem the first point we settle, with as much exactness as possible, is our objective." Ibid., 154.

Cf. also: C.H. Douglas, *Social Credit*, rev. ed. (New York: Gordon Press, 1933), 168:

"In considering the design, either of a mechanism or of an undertaking, it is first of all necessary to have a specific and well-defined objective, and, after that, a knowledge not only of the methods by which that objective can be obtained, but also of the nature and treatment of the forces which will be involved, the materials available, and their reaction to those forces."

[86] C.H. Douglas, *Warning Democracy*, 3rd ed. (London: Stanley Nott, 1931), 201.

[87] Ibid., 108.

Just so long as a rigid abstraction is made the test to which physical facts must conform ..., just so long must there be friction and abrasion between the theory and the facts (and facts are much harder than theories). Dissatisfaction and disappointment in the world as a result, can be predicted with certainty.[88]

The Nature of Morality

Morality deals with that part of the Canon which governs the selection of polices as well as of means from the point of view of what is in keeping with the fundamental meaning and ultimate purpose of being.[89] The moral 'ought' designates action which is in line with being at this deepest of levels and such action distinguishes itself practically from immoral forms of action because it is always the course of action which works best in maintaining, affirming, and promoting the reality of being. As Douglas once put it: "That is moral which works best."[90] Notice that Douglas did not say that the morally correct path coincides with that which works tolerably well, or that which works to some extent some of the time; rather, it is only that course of action which 'works best' which is said to be morally correct. In other words, morality is about choosing those courses of action that will release the goodness inherent in being to the greatest possible extent and that are therefore grounded on a fundamental respect for the true nature of reality.

Since the proximate end of human existence is self-development, there are certainly some actions which work best in facilitating that end and others which interfere with it. The same observation could be made *mutatis*

---

[88] C.H. Douglas, *Social Credit*, rev. ed. (New York: Gordon Press, 1933), 64.

[89] I would suggest that the ultimate purpose of being is communion with the Divine. Moral actions are those which facilitate and deepen this communion, whereas immoral actions weaken or destroy it.

[90] C.H. Douglas, *Credit-Power and Democracy* (Melbourne: The Social Credit Press, 1933), vii.

mutandis regarding the ultimate end of human existence. Without intending to reduce morality to a mere function of the individual's flourishing, it is nevertheless true that as a criterion for *identifying* which types of behaviours, attitudes, and actions are morally correct, this eudaemonistic perspective is most advantageous. That is, just as there are laws which govern the behaviour of bodies under the force of gravity, so too is there a law which governs deliberately chosen human action from the point of view of the true end of human nature. Conceived of in this manner, Douglas readily acknowledged the overriding importance of the moral point of view in evaluating human activity: "From many and varied quarters we receive proposals for lines of action which rely for their validity on an appeal to the moral law. Let us hasten to say that we have the greatest sympathy with this appeal."[91]

Obedience to the moral law is crucial from Douglas' assessment of human nature because it is, perhaps paradoxically, only by *freely* submitting to the moral law that the human being becomes a fully functional individual (since it is the law which stipulates the conditions for proper self-development): "*A mob has no morality; an individual depends for his individuality* on his morality. Lying and corruption disintegrate a man. No society can survive a-moral leadership."[92]

The claim that the prescriptions of genuine morality, once they are properly internalized, are not burdensome or oppressive but liberating and affirming is completely in line with the authentic Christian teaching on the nature of the moral law. True morality is not a heteronomous imposition from without, but an autonomous assimilation of the Canon from within. The proper spirit in which morality is to be understood and embraced was expressed quite well by Father John Walsh in his book *This is Catholicism*:

God is the expert on human life: He made it; He owns it; He knows what things benefit it and what things harm it. In the Ten Commandments, God shares this expert knowledge with us. The Commandments constitute, therefore, a succinct, clear manual of instructions showing us how to conduct our lives properly – what to do, what to avoid.

---

[91] C.H. Douglas, *The Development of World Dominion* (Sydney: Tidal Publications, 1969), 2.

[92] Ibid., 35.

Anyone remains free, of course, to disregard God's professional advice and to make up his own rule book. Such a method of acting, however, is most unintelligent. It is impossible to run the delicate, highpowered mechanism of a human life in defiance of its Author's directions. Anyone who tries it is due for a smashup.

Nor should it be thought that faithful obedience to God's commands results in a colorless, inhibited, unrewarding life. Although the phraseology employed in most of the Commandments is negative ("Thou shalt *not*") the intention underlying them is far from negative. Throughout the entire Decalogue, God is actually telling man how to get the most out of life, how to exploit all its precious possibilities, how to pursue it in a richly satisfying fashion – in harmony with Him, with one's neighbor, and with one's self. By forbidding us to do certain things, therefore, God intends not to curtail our happiness but to insure it; not to hamper freedom but to provide it with the widest area in which to operate; not to stifle self-expression but to guide us toward the fullest, most effective and enriching use of all our human faculties, our native powers and opportunities. God loves human life and wants us to reap the best possible advantages from the opportunity given us. That is why He proclaims the Ten Commandments.[93]

Since morality according to Douglas deals with laws which, like other laws of reality, 'transcend human thinking', morality possesses an objective significance: "... what I mean by good is something which is just as much in the nature of things, as gravity is in regard to physics."[94]

Just as there is canonical action (i.e., action in keeping with the Canon) within the moral sphere, there is also anti-canonical action. The objectivity of the moral law can be ascertained by observing that violations of that law bear real consequences where self-development is concerned.[95] While one

---

[93] John Walsh, *This is Catholicism* (Garden City, New York: Image Books, 1959), 46.

[94] C.H. Douglas, *The Policy of a Philosophy* (Vancouver: The Institute of Economic Democracy, 1977), 15-16.

[95] Douglas pointed out on a number of occasions that "there is no Law without a sanction." C.H. Douglas, *Realistic Constitutionalism* (London: K.R.P. Publications Ltd., 1947), 5. In the case of the moral law, the sanction consists in the consequences which, *inter alia*, moral transgression bears with respect to the self-development of the individual.

is free to disregard the moral law at one's convenience (unlike the laws of physics which are automatically compelling – one must obey them), one is not free to avoid the consequences of having disregarded the moral law.[96] For every moral transgression there is a corresponding punishment, even if this punishment might be a long time in coming: "the Mills of God grind very slowly, though they grind exceeding small."[97] An individual who habitually lies in order to manipulate others, for example, loses by degrees the capacity to discern the truth from falsehood and with it the ability to act effectively. In the same way, if a person freely chooses to violate the laws of physical health by not eating the right foods, not getting enough rest, or not exercising, etc., it is only a matter of time before this ill-treatment of his body will come back to haunt him. This presence in reality of an inborn sanction shows that true morality is not a matter of mere preference, custom, or political trickery, but is something inherent to the very nature of the world.

The conscious refusal to obey the moral law brings something new into existence: evil, which, alongside the good, is also an objective feature of the world. Douglas made his belief in the existence of evil clear when he criticized the widespread modern tendency to deny its reality:

> **One of the curious, not to say sinister, features of the current period is the prevalence of that form of Black Magic which consists in saying and affirming that evil does not exist. ...**
>
> **Nevertheless and notwithstanding, the Devil never did a cleverer piece of work than when he persuaded his victims that he does not exist.**
>
> **The proofs of it are everywhere. The growing inability to distinguish good from evil, with its corollary that nothing matters, there are no objectives except the whim of the moment (and the whims themselves are giving out), no absolute values; nothing is "proper",**

---

[96] One of these consequences of disregarding the authentic laws of the universe is the fact that disobedience eventually makes us enslaved; i.e., freely electing to disobey these laws actually destroys over time our very capacity to act freely or independently of external causes. In this way, immorality makes it more and more difficult to actualize the faculty of free will as our disordered desires begin to control us more effectively than we can constrain them.

[97] C.H. Douglas, *The Realistic Position of the Church of England* (Liverpool: K.R.P. Publications Ltd., 1948), 13.

therefore there is no property; that since it is now much easier (temporarily) to vote yourself into your neighbour's house than to build one for yourself, work is foolish and politics without preparation is the universal career. These are the logical outcome of a crude *mono-theism.*

The combined inability and unwillingness of so many of the pseudo-educated, firstly to recognise the wave of Evil which is sweeping the world, and secondly to realise the extent to which its Servants rely upon absence of publicity and criticism is a major factor in the spiritual Armageddon which is in progress. It is becoming increasingly true that only one metaphysic, dialectal materialism, is presented, in various forms, to a conditioned majority: (nothing could be more remarkable, outside a Russian "Trial", than the acceptance of responsibility for the present chaos by those who are the greatest sufferers by it). Good and evil have no place in this; Power is Lord of all.

The denial of evil is an affirmation of equality – having no quality. This is the end of entropy unmodified – Power which renders itself powerless.[98]

Very often, evil takes the form of treating what is, in reality, a mere means *as if* it were an end in itself, in which case the authentic end is reduced to something that is dispensable: "the tragedy of human effort ... arises more than from any other single cause from a failure to distinguish between means and ends, amounting in many cases to the elevation of what are only means to ends in themselves."[99] In a like manner, St. Athanasius held that confusing means with ends is of the very essence of sin.[100] The consequence of abusing a means in this way is an ever greater dissatisfaction borne of an ever-intensifying dysfunction:

---

[98] C.H. Douglas, *The Development of World Dominion* (Sydney: Tidal Publications, 1969), 8-9.

[99] C.H. Douglas, *The Tragedy of Human Effort* (Vancouver: The Institute of Economic Democracy, 1978), 9.

[100] Cf. Eric de Maré, *A Matter of Life or Debt* (Bullsbrook, Western Australia: Veritas Publishing Company Pty. Ltd., 1985), 42.

It appears to be in the nature of the Universe that the misuse of a "means" results in the breakdown of the means misused.[101]

Do we live, for example, in order to work or do we work in order to live? The consequence of regarding life as a mere means to economic employment (work in the narrowest of senses) often involves compromising the spiritual, psychological, and physical well-being of the worker. Together with his early demise, these other losses follow as due penalties for having made or having been forced to make the wrong choice.

A second example of this pattern of inverting means with ends would be the tendency of totalitarian, authoritarian, and false democracies to subordinate individuals, who are the true ends which associations should serve, to government and its institutions. They erroneously treat individuals as a mere means and institutions as ends in themselves:

The first step towards the security of the individual is to insist upon the security of the individual. I hope that is not too difficult to understand. If you place the security of any institution before the security of the individual, you may prolong the life of that institution, but you will certainly shorten the lives of a great many individuals. Institutions are means to an end, and I do not think it is too much to say that the elevation of means into ends, of institutions above humanity, constitutes an unforgiveable sin, in the pragmatic sense that it brings upon itself the most tremendous penalties that life contains.[102]

Subordinating ends to means instead of means to ends is such a common phenomenon where evil is concerned (various examples of it appear throughout Social Credit literature) that Douglas regularly invoked an

---

[101] C.H. Douglas, *"Whose Service is Perfect Freedom"* (Bullsbrook, Western Australia: 1983), 5. Treating a means as if it were an end in itself is the essential nature of 'perversion'. Sadly, many spheres of contemporary human life are infected with perversions of various kinds: "As my experience grows, I am increasingly confident that one, at least, of the key words leading to an understanding of the conscious Evil Forces in this world, is 'perversion'." C.H. Douglas, *The Big Idea* (Bullsbrook, Australia: Veritas Publishing Company, 1983), 13.

[102] C.H. Douglas, *Security Institutional and Personal* (Liverpool: K.R.P. Publications Ltd., 1945), 8.

ancient aphorism to describe it: *Demon est Deus inversus* – the devil is God upside down.[103]

Another key manifestation of evil for Douglas is the disorder which ensues whenever an intrinsically evil means is employed in the pursuit of a good end. In this particular case, there is no confusion and consequent inversion regarding what it is that is to serve as the means and what it is that is to serve as the end; rather, the means chosen is a bad one because it violates the moral law in its very essence. It must be pointed out that the use of an intrinsically evil means is something which can and has been employed by both 'liberal' as well as 'conservative' political forces; i.e., it is not merely those who are left-wing on social policies who have been guilty of doing evil so that good might come from it. To cite just one example of a 'right-wing' policy which involves an intrinsically evil means, Douglas is on record as arguing that impertinent prohibitions on the production and sale of alcoholic products are not a morally acceptable means for dealing with the problems caused by drunkenness:

The courageous bishop who stated that he would rather see England free than sober, may, or may not, have realised that he was postulating in an attractive form, an issue which challenges the idea that a good end can excuse a bad means.[104]

An original defence of the principle that 'the end does not justify the means' could be extrapolated from Douglas' general thinking as follows: firstly let it be observed that: "It is undeniable that every action has consequences."[105] Furthermore, not only does every action have consequences, but we also "know that over every plane of action with which

---

[103] While it appears that this statement is originally derived, *via* theosophy, from kabbalistic thought, Douglas must have intended it in a Christian sense; i.e., evil is typically an inversion of the good or due order, just as Satan can be thought of as embodying an unjustified inversion of the moral principles of the divinity. However, as one of Douglas' close collaborators, Geoffrey Dobbs, has explained, when taken in its most literal sense the statement is not true. Contrary to the kabbalistic idea that Satan and evil in general are co-equal with God and goodness as an inherent part of reality (along the lines of 'as above, so below'), Dobbs correctly pointed out that "the devil is not God – even upside down." Cf. http://www.alor.org/Library/Dobbs%20G%20-%20The%20Douglas%20Legacy.htm

[104] C.H. Douglas, *Social Credit*, rev. ed. (New York: Gordon Press, 1973), 10.

[105] Ibid., 38.

we are acquainted, action and reaction are equal, opposite, and wholly automatic."[106] This equal, opposite, and wholly automatic reaction is not necessarily immediate, however. Thus we see that using a means which is at odds with morality, i.e., at odds with what works best in forwarding the true end of human existence (of which self-development is an integral part), can only lead to the production of a reaction which is equal, opposite, and wholly automatic, and, as such, 'doing evil so that some kind of good can come from it' is invariably bound to be counter-productive to such an extent that it is hardly worth the effort:

A given line of action, dictated by immediate expediency, may appear to be beneficial; but the subsequent result may be found to have intensified the evil. A severe pain may be alleviated by opium; but an opium habit is almost certainly deadly.[107]

In keeping with the adage that 'God always forgives, people sometimes forgive, but nature never forgives', there is a price to be paid for every violation of the authentic moral order such that a good end cannot ever excuse an evil means in a very real *pragmatic* sense (even apart from more theoretical or principled considerations).

A third form of evil that crops up quite frequently might be described as 'trespass' or the assumption of the right to determine policy in a realm that lies beyond one's due sovereignty. Anyone who serves a legitimate function in a society should certainly have sufficient power and authority to fulfill that function well. However, whenever such an individual or group of individuals wish to go beyond the due limits of their function (by using the power inherent in their function as a type of fulcrum by means of which they aim to control the decisions of their subordinates concerning things that are none of their business and are irrelevant to the fulfillment of their duties), they are usurping a power which does not belong to them in the nature of things. In this sense, the theory and practice of trespass is in direct opposition to the principle of subsidiarity.

---

[106] Ibid., 31.

[107] C.H. Douglas, *The Realistic Position of the Church of England* (Liverpool: K.R.P. Publications Ltd., 1948), 13.

Morality vs. Moralism

True morality must be clearly differentiated with what might be termed 'moralism'. There is a counterfeit moral ethos which employs the metaphysical gravity implicit in moral questions as a type of leverage by means of which individuals can be pressured to pursue courses of action that are, in fact, not in their authentic best interests at all. It is often possible, by means of abstract moral reasoning, to justify conduct which, when evaluated realistically, reveals itself to be immoral as a matter of fact. In such a case, one is strenuously advocating in the name of morality some action or set of actions that do not work best in practice. A good example of the moralistic approach is the typical 'morality' of the Whig:

[T]he keynote of Whig policy ... is hypocrisy – the justification, on some allegedly moral ground, of policies which are in fact not merely narrowly selfish, but pragmatically disastrous.[108]

A key component of 'moralism', then, is its tendency to conceive of morality in abstract terms in line with some deductive conception of the moral sphere in opposition to what the laws of morality show themselves to be inductively on the basis of lived experience. The approach of moralism to the datum of morality is, in fact, an application of the anti-phenomenological methodological approach which subordinates reality to abstractions, whereas Douglas' conception of morality is grounded in the key phenomenological claim that abstractions should be subordinated to reality.

A distinction must therefore be made between the abstract morality of 'moralism' and true morality which is concrete or realistic in nature. An abstract principle of distributive justice, for example, is a conception of 'fairness' in keeping with some deductive theory of moral values. It is based on the idealistic ought and as such the pattern of distribution of harms and benefits which it prescribes is necessarily at odds with the course of action which would really maximize a state of well-being for all of the interested parties. The idealistic approach demonstrates: "the futility

---

[108] C.H. Douglas, "Money: An Historical Survey", *The Fig Tree* No. 2 (September 1936), 140.

of abstract justice when in opposition to the solid facts of life."[109] Concrete justice, by contrast, refers to that pattern of distribution of harms and benefits which shows itself in practice to work, not tolerably, not well, but best. It is based on the application of the realistic ought. This is the test which Douglas adopted when considering the moral integrity of economic arrangements:

> **[W]hile society is justified – *i.e.*, is judicious – in demanding that this machine shall be operated by those capable of obtaining the best results from it, irrespective of any other considerations whatever, society as a whole, not the operators – Labour – or any other function of society, has a "right" to the product, a "right" founded in the nature of things because, if it is denied, the machine begins to develop abnormal friction, with a consequent loss to every constituent member of society.[110]**

Morality and Progress

In the modern world, we have a tendency to assume that all technical progress is somehow unqualifiedly good simply because it involves an advance in the application of knowledge and materials. On the contrary, the only type of technical progress which could be considered good from a moral standpoint and hence worthy of civilization is that type of progress which enables us to better serve the right objectives, i.e., those which are grounded on a true 'philosophy' and are therefore consonant with the objective nature of reality. The development of better tools only deserves to be regarded as a manifestation of authentic progress if such development makes it easier for us to achieve a state of well-being both individually and collectively:

---

[109] C.H. Douglas, *Social Credit*, rev. ed. (New York: Gordon Press, 1973), 71. Cf. also page 64 of the same work: "Just so long as a rigid abstraction is made the test to which physical facts must conform ..., just so long must there be friction and abrasion between theory and facts (and facts are much harder than theories). Dissatisfaction and disappointment in the word as a result, can be predicted with certainty."

[110] C.H. Douglas, *Credit Power and Democracy* (Melbourne: The Social Credit Press, 1933), 19.

It has been our habit to flatter ourselves that during the past 150 years or so we have made great progress, and we have used the word 'progress' as though it defined itself. Now the fact is, that nearly all of what we call progress is a-moral. Or to put the matter another way, there is no moral progress except moral progress, and the use of better tools in no way ensures better objectives. In the main, the period under review is characterised by a superficial acceleration in the achievement of vague objectives. We have cut down the time required to travel from Europe to North America from three weeks to ten hours.

What do we do with the time we have saved? Our houses (some of them) are lit by the pressing of a button. Do we find them more pleasant than the houses of the sixteenth century lit by candles? We call this a labour-saving age. In the fourteenth century there were ninety statutory holidays per annum, and the idea of "work" was completely alien to a large part of the population. Six hundred years ago, there were no police, and no police would have been tolerated. Was there more crime than at the present time? There is no evidence of it.

... civilisation ... is a misnomer unless it involves moral progress. ....

Now the only rational meaning which can be attached to the phrase "moral progress" is firstly a continuous approach to Reality (which includes and perhaps is, real Politics), and secondly, the ordering of our actions, in the light of such approach, so that they tend towards our own and the general good. And if, as may be held, Reality and Good, or God, are synonymous, these two come to much the same thing.[111]

We must also add that there is no historical evidence to suggest that progress, whether technical or moral, is either necessarily inevitable or automatic.

---

[111] C.H. Douglas, *"Whose Service is Perfect Freedom"* (Bullsbrook, Western Australia: 1983), 10, 12.

Morality and Power

Finally, it behooves us to examine the oft repeated claim that, in the real world, 'might is stronger than right' and that this is an important fact which people must accept and one to which they must adapt themselves if they wish to survive and prosper. While admitting that in many cases considerations of pure power do outweigh moral considerations in practice, Douglas pointed out that it is also a fact that the most powerful actions possible are those which combine right and might: righteous might is stronger than unrighteous might because the former is in full conformity with the laws which govern reality:

> **In this world it is action which counts. The only sense in which the phrase "Right is stronger than Might" is anything but pernicious nonsense is that, in the last event, might depends on the actions of individuals, and if it is possible to affect the actions of individuals by something which we call "Right," "Might" and "Right" may eventually be found on the same side.**[112]

Religion and the Application of the Canon

We have already seen how, with regards to any particular issue or problem, there are a variety of different policies (many of them incompatible) which can be adopted. This diversity forces us to make choices and hence the need for a principle by means of which the 'correct' policy or set of policies can be selected. Such a principle would constitute an arch-policy or a 'policy concerning policies' and would mirror in the sphere of action the role which the phenomenological criterion for the discernment of truth plays as the criterion of criteria in the sphere of cognition.

In seeking to identify what this correct arch-policy might happen to be, Douglas examined the word 'religion' in terms of its etymology and noted

---

[112] C.H. Douglas, *Social Credit*, rev. ed. (New York: Gordon Press, 1933), 170-171. It is also true that there is a heavy price to be paid whenever individuals or groups of people decide to separate 'might' from what is 'right'. Superficially 'might' may be stronger than 'right', but every victory of 'might' divorced from 'right' only prepares for its progenitors a new and more devastating defeat in the long run. 'Blowback' is a phenomenon which can assume many different forms.

that it comes from a word meaning to bind back or to bind and that it is related to the word 'ligament'.[113] Taking its etymological origin into consideration, it is not surprising that one key aspect of any religious worldview, or better put, the religious existential condition, is the impelling belief that what one does should be a function of, or in conformity with, what one holds to be real. Reality and reality alone should determine one's overall life-policy. It is in this very narrow sense that religion may be defined as "any sort of doctrine which is based on an attempt to relate action to some conception of reality."[114] Religiously motivated action is action which involves "the binding back either of action, or of policy ... to reality."[115] 'Binding back' is to be understood as "to bring into close relation again, ..."[116] In other words, the religious outlook insists that policy must be grounded in a correct 'philosophy', i.e., one that corresponds to reality. Might should be oriented by what is right, because that is what works best.

Now the religious attitude to policy is correct insofar as it recognizes the true principle that action and hence policy should always be grounded in and based upon reality (not fantasy). *It is only when policy is based on reality, as opposed to a false vision of that reality which happens to pander to a desire for convenience, comfort, expediency, or power, etc., that intended results may be achieved in the easiest possible way.* In other words, the authentic religious mindset rightly contends that policy should be governed by the prescriptions of the realistic ought. Douglas was quick to note, however, that attempting to base policy on reality does not guarantee that one's conception of reality, or one's 'philosophy', is actually correct. It is therefore crucial that one's religious zeal in seeking to relate action to some conception of reality be actually grounded in a *correct* conception of reality.

---

[113] Cf. C.H. Douglas, *The Policy of a Philosophy* (Vancouver: The Institute of Economic Democracy, 1977), 2.

[114] Ibid., 2. Douglas admitted that this was a narrow definition of religion as he made it clear in the same address that he was defining the term for his own specific purpose.

[115] Ibid., 2.

[116] Ibid., 2.

The harm which has been done by well-intentioned but misdirected religious zeal, i.e., enthusiasm for action which is falsely believed to be 'right', has been very great indeed. A stubborn adherence to a set of what are, in fact, idealistic oughts has often served as the driving force behind counter-productive 'fundamentalisms' and hidebound attitudes of every type – whether these be religious in the strictest sense or merely ideo-logical in character – to the very great dissatisfaction of all concerned. The well-meaning individuals who are caught in this web become unwitting but faithful servants of dysfunction, whence the aphorism: 'the road to hell is paved with good intentions.'

In spite of this perennial danger, let us be careful not to throw the baby out with the bath water. We cannot avoid acting and so we cannot ignore the questions as to whether there is something real (something which exists independently of our thoughts and perceptions) and whether or not our action should be based on it. The very fact that, in many distinct cases, action which has been shown to be in line with reality has produced stupendous results that could not have been produced otherwise validates the claim that policy should be based on a correct conception of what is real; i.e., the religious outlook on the question of policy is sound in form if not always in content.[117] The whole problem of authentic progress in what-ever field of human endeavour revolves around the "problem of making the world a closer approach to reality ..."[118], of aligning policy with the nature of reality in keeping with the prescriptions of the realistic ought. It is for this reason and in this particular sense that the Social Credit worldview is correctly described as a religious worldview:

It appears to us to be axiomatic that (what, in fact, its experts have always contended) religion, in the sense of a binding back of life to reality, is of primary importance. Until you have some kind of re-liable chart, you are a mere waif on the ocean. Clearly religion in

---

[117] Ibid., 15: "To my mind, the whole thing depends upon this question of reality. If you are working in accordance with something which is real (and when I say real, I mean something which is in the nature of the universe, in the same way as the law of gravity is in the nature of the universe), you will get results which cannot be got even if you are working along proper lines for something which is unreal."

[118] C.H. Douglas, *The Approach to Reality* (London: K.R.P. Publications Ltd., 1936), 7.

this sense is a seven-days-a-week matter, and requires to be distinguished carefully from "good conduct". It ought to result in good conduct, and in fact be the only test of good conduct, but that is something else again.[119]

By contrast, any individual or group which, for whatever reason, insists on basing policy on what is convenient, comfortable, or otherwise expedient, rather than on what is real, might rightly be described not as religious (i.e., authentically progressive) but rather as reactionary.

---

[119] C.H. Douglas, *The Development of World Dominion* (Sydney: Tidal Publications, 1969), 19-20.

Chapter Four: The Social Philosophy of Social Credit

It is upon entering into a discussion of the social philosophy of Social Credit that we encounter the very heart of Social Credit theory. The relationship existing between the individual and the group constitutes its material or topical focal point:

> As I conceive it, Social Credit covers and comprehends a great deal more than the money problem. Important as that is, primarily important because it is a question of priority, Social Credit fundamentally involves a conception, I feel a true conception – but you must enlarge upon that for yourselves – of the relationships between individuals and their association in countries and nations, between individuals and their association in groups.[120]

So many of our political, economic, and indeed cultural problems stem from a lack of accurate and complete knowledge concerning the *due relation* which should obtain between individuals and the groups of which they form a part. To some extent, this ignorance has even been excusable because the analytical and evaluative tasks of the science of association are not nearly as straightforward or as simple as one might think:

> There is probably no more subtle and elusive subject than the consideration of the exact relation of the group in all these and countless other forms, to the individuals who compose the groups.[121]

---

[120] C.H. Douglas, *The Approach to Reality* (London: K.R.P. Publications Ltd., 1936), 6. The fact that the financial remedies put forward by Douglas and commonly associated in the popular imagination with 'Social Credit' were always and only a *means* to a much more important end was underscored by Douglas in the following terms: "The set of ideas which became the movement known as Social Credit began with an examination of the problem of the relationship of the individual to the group, and the financial proposals which emerged were consciously, and in all their developments, designed to free the individual from group domination." C.H. Douglas, *The Development of World Dominion* (Sydney: Tidal Publications, 1969), 1.

[121] C.H. Douglas, *Social Credit*, rev. ed. (New York: Gordon Press, 1933), 27.

The whole purpose of the social philosophy of Social Credit is to clearly unveil to a long-suffering humanity the basic directives of the Canon with respect to associations.

The General Nature of Association

In approaching this particular subject, let us take as our point of departure the observation that human individuals, like many other life forms, exhibit a strong tendency to associate themselves into groups in order to make it easier for them to attain certain objectives:

> **It appears to be a fundamental instinct of conscious life, well developed even in the animal kingdom, that certain advantages can be gained by the association of individuals into a group, which cannot be attained in other ways. It is equally true that in a primitive state of existence the advantages of the group carry with them definite disadvantages to the individual. It is true that many hands make light work, but it is not less true that he travels the fastest who travels alone.[122]**

Insofar as association renders it easier or even possible to attain certain ends, the power gained represents an *increment* of association; and, insofar as the requirements of an association burden an individual, the power lost represents a *decrement* of association as far as that same individual is concerned. Douglas understood that depending on the nature and the extent of the increments and corresponding decrements which are characteristic of a particular type of association, the organization of individuals into a group may tend in the direction of being either a blessing or a curse for the individuals who compose it: "Association is at once the direct cause of our progress and of our threatened destruction."[123]

Whether or not a given association happens to be a blessing or a curse for this or that particular member is dependent on the formal structure of the association. That structure is largely a function of the overarching policy which governs the association, and, like any other policy, it must be

---

[122] C.H. Douglas, *The Monopoly of Credit*, 4th ed. (Sudbury: Bloomfield Books, 1979), 11.

[123] C.H. Douglas, *The Tragedy of Human Effort* (Vancouver: The Institute of Economic Democracy, 1978), 2.

be based on some 'philosophy'. In this case, the underlying 'philosophy' has to do with a conception of the proper relations which should exist between individuals and their groups.

The 'Philosophies' behind Association

There are, at bottom, two basic 'philosophies' which are operative in the world where the relations between individuals and their associations are concerned. These two 'philosophies' are mutually exclusive and they give birth to conflicting policies.

The first 'philosophy' is the one which serves as the basis for every form of despotism. It claims that all social power, i.e., the ability to get things done in association, originates *outside* of the individual or is *external* to him. As a result, the lone individual is considered as being less important than the group, and it is therefore to the group that the individual and his autonomous interests should be subordinated. Given the metaphysical priority of the group, the individual must have policies imposed on him in order to make him do whatever is claimed to be in the best interests of the group.[124] He is thus regarded as part of a mob who can be adequately catered to on the basis of statistics, as raw material for the planning exercised by those who, on account of their favourable position in the social hierarchy, wield the levers of centralized social power. The individual is not to be trusted to use his individual powers in a socially responsible way and so they must be taken from him and transferred to an elite who claim to know what is ultimately good for the individual.

The second 'philosophy' is the one which nourishes the authentically democratic spirit. It affirms that all social power arises from *within* the individual. The group is therefore inferior to the individual and indeed only exists to serve the individual. Since the whole purpose of group activity is to help the individual consolidate and extend the individual power to which he has access in order that he might better achieve his own ends, the only acceptable limitations or demands which can be imposed on the individual are those which coincide with the genuine *functional* necessities of the association in question, i.e., those which arise in view of this purpose. Beyond these warranted limitations or legitimate expectations,

---

[124] More often than not what the individual is forced to do on the basis of this type of 'philosophy' is not so much in the best interests of the group, but rather in the best interests of the elite few who control the group. The usual plea "it's for the good of all" is merely a guise.

the individual has certain God-given and hence inalienable rights which can never be legitimately violated by any group association to which he may belong.[125]

The Different Types of Associations

The Analysis of Formal Structures

The two 'philosophies' of association, the philosophy of non-immanent social power and the philosophy of immanent social power, are mirrored at the level of policy by what might be termed the policy of domination, which is nourished by the 'will-to-power', on the one hand, and the policy of freedom, which is animated by the 'will-to-freedom' on the other:

There are only two Great Policies in the world to-day – Domination and Freedom. Any policy which aims at the establishment of a complete sovereignty, whether it be of a Kaiser, a League, a State, a Trust, or a Trade Union, is a policy of Domination, irrespective of the fine words with which it may be accompanied; and any policy which makes it easier for the individual to benefit by association, without being constrained beyond the inherent necessities of the function involved in the association, is a policy of Freedom.[126]

---

[125] The conflict existing between these two 'philosophies' bears a great metaphysical and hence historical importance: "Probably the future of humanity turns on the answer to a single question: Does Social Power proceed from within, or does it reside in guns, tanks and aeroplanes [i.e., does it proceed from without – OH]?" C.H. Douglas, *The Big Idea* (Bullsbrook, Australia: Veritas Publishing Company, 1983), 65.

[126] C.H. Douglas, *These Present Discontents and The Labour Party and Social Credit* (London: Cecil Palmer, 1922), 5. It may be opportune to clarify the notion of functional necessity. From the Social Credit point of view, the only limitations on individual freedom that can be justified by the inherent nature of things are those regulations that are shown to be required in practice to produce the complete and effective subordination of the group to the individual. The individual freedom which Social Credit advocates is not libertarian freedom, however; i.e., there is never a right to interfere with or disregard those regulations or responsibilities which are necessary, on account of the nature of reality, to maximize the benefits of group association for *each* individual to the greatest extent possible. While it is true that what might count as appropriate regulations will likely differ depending on time and place, that these should always be kept to the minimum that is needed, and that they should be summarily discarded once they are no longer required, there are indeed restrictions, which, being grounded in the Canon, reveal themselves as authoritative if the true purpose of association (as envisaged by the democratic model of association) is to be adequately fulfilled.

Depending on the particular policy that an association adopts, the association will have one of two distinct types of structures. At issue is whether the individual is to be considered as a means to a greater or lesser degree and the group as a legitimate end in and of itself, or whether the individual is and can only be regarded as an end in himself with the group only ever operating as a pure means for the sake of his advancement.

Associations which are constructed in keeping with the policy of domination possess *despotic* structures: the individual is subordinated to the group to a greater or lesser extent, while associations which are constructed in keeping with the policy of freedom possess genuinely *democratic* structures: the group is thoroughly subordinated to the individual.[127] The subordination of the individual to the group means that the individual, at any rate the common individual, is regarded as something which, to one degree or another, exists to serve the alleged interests of the group. The association is centrifugal. The opposite arrangement, i.e., the subordination of the group to the individual, views the group and group activity as a mere means to advance the well-being of each and every individual member; the association is at the complete service of the individual.[128] This type of association is centripetal.

The correct set of regulations is not, therefore, a matter of mere preference or arbitrary choice; it must be discovered and then applied in practice. It is certainly possible that disagreements amongst people of good faith may arise concerning what the correct regulations actually happen to be, but this fact should not cause us to abandon the will either to implement or maintain whatever shows itself to be a correct regulatory principle. Any disputes of this type should be settled by free inquiry and debate and, if necessary, trial and error.

[127] N.B. , the terms 'despotic' and 'democratic' are being used here in a *structural* as opposed to a political sense. It is perfectly possible for an association such as a family, for example, to be structurally democratic (i.e., with the group serving the well-being of each individual member) while being political authoritarian with the father as its head. At the same time, it is also possible for an association such as a nation to be ostensibly democratic politically, while actually possessing a despotic structure to a greater or lesser extent (i.e., with the individual being subordinated, in various ways and to various degrees, to the group).

[128] On this view, "institutions exist only legitimately to serve individuals, ..." C.H. Douglas, *The Big Idea* (Bullsbrook, Australia: Veritas Publishing Company, 1983), 69.

These two conceptions of the due relation which ought to obtain between individuals and their groups are diametrically opposed and are thus irreconcilable. Any failure on the part of an association to fully embody a democratic structure tends, therefore, in the direction of despotism. The most extreme despotic structure imaginable would be that which Orwell referred to as 'oligarchical collectivism' or, in other words, the worst possible form of totalitarianism.[129] In a totalitarian association, the individual is subordinated to the group to the greatest extent that this is physically or objectively possible without destroying or completely neutralizing the individual and his activity, although, in some cases, he might even be *obligated* to sacrifice himself for the sake of the group. All associations, whether they be political, economic, or cultural in nature, can therefore be placed on a continuum between an association which, on the one hand, is as totalitarian as physical limitations will permit, and an association which embodies, as perfectly as possible, a democratic structure on the other:

Totalitarian Structure---Democratic Structure

Increasingly despotic

Successful democratic associations, i.e., those which effectively subordinate the group to the individual, consistently deliver a certain result: they maximize to the greatest desirable extent possible the benefits of association for each individual by maximizing the increments of association for that individual while simultaneously minimizing the decrements. This requires, in turn, that no artificial limits be placed on the benefits that can be derived from the unearned increment of association and that these benefits be distributed equitably (not necessarily equally) to all of the individual members of the association. In a democratically structured association that has also adopted the appropriate means of implementation, the individual is able to obtain the desired benefits while only contributing that which is absolutely necessary (on account of the inherent nature of things) for the attainment of this objective. The fulfillment of this objective embodies the greatest possible freedom for the 'individual-in-association'.

---

[129] Cf. George Orwell, *1984* (New York: Plume, 1983), especially 163-193.

Successful despotic associations, by contrast, i.e., those which effectively subordinate individuals to the group by using the best means available for that particular purpose, fail to deliver the same highly satisfactory result. The greater the extent of the failure, the greater is the degree of despotism which characterizes the association. Instead of maximizing the increments of association while minimizing the decrements of association to the desirable extent possible for each individual member, such associations maximize the increments of association and minimize the decrements of association for the sake of the abstract collectivity, or for the majority of individuals, or, more frequently in practice, for the interests of the minority controlling the group. In each of these instances the despotic association is putting the alleged interests of the group ahead of the interests of the sovereign individual.[130] The fulfillment of this alternative objective thus embodies a greater or lesser degree of enslavement as far as the common individual is concerned.

Given the diametrically opposed nature of their overriding objectives, there are, not surprisingly, a number of other characteristics which are uniquely associated with the despotic association in comparison with its democratic counterpart and *vice versa*.

The Centralization vs. the Decentralization of Power

The despotic model of association naturally tends to centralize power to ever greater degrees. Since it is built on the belief that all social power arises from outside of the individual, it would seem to follow that the more control over this power can be placed in the hands of a few, the greater will be the facility with which this elite can produce the intended results of association. The increasing centralization of this power is complemented, on the side of the individual, by an ever increasing degree of servility. It is for this reason that the despotic association is the servile association. The democratic model of association, by contrast, tends in the opposite direction, i.e., it favours the maximum decentralization of power possible. Personal sovereignty, i.e., individual control over policy, must be respected

---

[130] In speaking of the 'sovereign individual', I am not speaking of an absolute sovereignty, but rather of a sovereignty within due limits.

and maintained to the full extent that individual freedom is compatible with the functional necessities of the association.[131]

Compulsion vs. Inducement

Despotically structured associations count on methods of compulsion (in keeping with the spirit of the 'will-to-power') in order that the association might function as directed by those elite few who occupy the apex of power. Democratically structured associations, on the other hand, rely on inducement as much as possible to obtain the co-operation of their individual members. This latter approach is very much in line with the spirit of the 'will-to-freedom' because it appeals to the ontological dignity of the individual (a dignity which is grounded in his rationality and freedom) in order to get things done: "inducement derives from within, from the individual, while compulsion is from without, from the 'machine'."[132]

Another important aspect of the difference between the method of compulsion and the method of inducement is that compulsion requires that discipline be imposed on individuals from without, whereas inducement calls forth a superior kind of discipline, one that is voluntarily submitted to or self-imposed.

Subordinating Individuality to the Environment vs. Subordinating the Environment to Individuality

A third distinction between the despotic and democratic models of association can be drawn by considering the particular type of relationship between the individual and his environment which each model promotes. While both recognize that the efficacy and efficiency of an association's ac-

---

[131] Decentralizing power to each individual (in whatever specific form an association seeks to deliver benefits to its membership) to the greatest extent possible is one way of maximizing individual freedom: *"power to make decisions is freedom for the individual, ..."* C.H. Douglas, *Credit Power and Democracy* (Melbourne: The Social Credit Press, 1933), 6.

[132] C.H. Douglas, *Credit Power and Democracy* (Melbourne: The Social Credit Press, 1933), 62. A little later on in this same chapter Douglas added the following observation: "inducement is inherently stronger than compulsion, or, as the older psychology would have it, ... love is stronger than fear, ..." C.H. Douglas, *Credit Power and Democracy* (Melbourne: The Social Credit Press, 1933), 65.

tivities is dependent on bringing human nature and its environment, and, in particular, the social environment created by the association, into alignment, the approaches which the two models take with respect to this task are diametrically opposed. The despotic model seeks to bring human nature into alignment with the environment by attempting to change human nature into that form which will suit the kind of social environment which despotic associations create; i.e., it tries to make human nature fit the type of world it thinks ought to be. In other words, the individual is subordinated to the environment on the basis of an idealistic ought. The democratic model, by contrast, recognizes the impossibility of trying to change human nature in any substantial sense and attempts, instead, to bring the environment into line with human nature by changing and improving the social environment so that it is reflective of what human beings deeply desire and value for themselves and their lives. By applying the approach of the realistic ought, the environment is subordinated to individuality. The paradox here is that by improving the environment it is possible to achieve changes in human behaviour which may be just as drastic as what could be achieved if it were truly possible and desirable to alter human nature itself:

> What, I think, is incontestably true is that the great underlying forces which inspire human nature to action do not change substantially, at any rate within the widest period of history which we can span, although, like everything else, they may be subject to evolution and they may change the forms of their expression. A recognition of the truth of this is, I think, the shortest answer to proposals which involve for their acceptance a radical change in human nature. We can re-group these forces and we can so alter their reaction to circumstances that we can achieve results just as radical as if we had changed the very nature of the forces, but this can only be done by an understanding of these forces and a conscious use of them rather than a wholly unscientific attempt to change their nature.[133]

---

[133] C.H. Douglas, *Major C.H. Douglas Speaks* (Sydney: Douglas Social Credit Association, 1933), 46-47.

It was with this surprising phenomenon in mind that the British Social Crediter, Eric de Maré, once proclaimed that "changed conditions change men."[134] While it is not possible to substantially alter human nature (and let it be recalled that attempts to do so have been productive of untold misery), the ability to adapt to changing conditions is nevertheless an important attribute of that nature. Given the right changes in the environment we can expect to consistently bring out the best qualities in human beings rather than the worst.

The Evaluation of Formal Structures

Having analyzed the two basic formal structures that an association can assume, it now becomes possible to evaluate them *from the point of view of the true purpose of any and every association*. Which of the two models aims at the true end of association? Which of these two models represents the correct formal structure which associations should seek to embody? We are faced with the choice between subordinating the individual to the group to a greater or lesser extent (the despotic model), or thoroughly subordinating the group to the individual (the democratic model). If the first 'philosophy' regarding the relationship existing between the individual and the group is correct, then the despotic model is the model which will work best. If the second 'philosophy' is correct, then the democratic model is the one which should be preferred. Determining which of these formal structures gives rise to the blessing and which one leads to the curse is a key evaluative or normative task of any social philosophy:

[A]s far as it is possible to sum the matter up, the general problem seems to be involved in a decision as to whether the individual should be sacrificed to the group or whether the fruits of group activity should be always at the disposal of the individual.[135]

---

[134] Eric de Maré, *A Matter of Life and Debt* (Bullsbrook, Australia: Veritas Publishing Company Pty. Ltd., 1985), 24.

[135] C.H. Douglas, *Social Credit*, rev. ed. (New York: Gordon Press, 1973), 27-28. Douglas was convinced that it is upon the discovery of the correct answer to this question that the solution to many of our earthly problems depends:

"Salvation is not to be found in greater and still greater agglomerations of power ...

The Correct Purpose of Association

Every association can only exist if it exists for *some* purpose. The *true* purpose of association, however, is the common good. The particular manifestation of the common good which a given association seeks to maximize is dependent on the type of association in question (whether it be political, economic, or cultural).

With respect to these first three propositions there is complete agreement between the despotic and the democratic models of association. The two models part ways, however, when it comes to determining how the common good is to be concretely understood. The despotic model envisions the common good as referring to the well-being of the society or association considered collectively, i.e., the well-being of the group taken as a whole, or from the point of view of the majority of its members, whereas the democratic model conceives of the common good as referring to the well-being of the society or association considered distributively, i.e., as the well-being of each individual. The question as to which model is the correct model for associations can thereby be reduced to the question of which model is built on the correct understanding of the common good and therefore aims to fulfill the true purpose of association.

The fact that the distributivistic understanding of the common good constitutes the correct understanding of the common good, and hence that the democratic model is the correct model for associations, can be demonstrated on a practical level by considering that any association which adequately fulfills the common good in the distributivistic sense is fundamentally stable, whereas any association which fails to fulfill the common good in the distributivistic sense is, to the extent that it fails, unstable.[136] In line with a general observation that Douglas once made: "human beings [are] anxious to gain their legitimate ends by the most

---

It is, and can only be found, in bringing into actuality the existing cleavage between the individual desire to pursue an individual end and the group pressure to reduce the individual to an amorphous mass – a biological entropy." C.H. Douglas, *The Brief for the Prosecution* (Liverpool: K.R.P. Publications Ltd., 1945), 63.

[136] In other words, the democratic model of association reveals itself as the correct model because it is the one which works best; it is "the only solution having inherent stability." C.H. Douglas, *Economic Democracy*, 5th ed. (Sudbury: Bloomfield Books, 1974), 117. Peace is the fruit of order and social stability is the result of the realistic integration of the proper means and ends where the activities of an association are concerned.

convenient and comfortable methods"[137], it should come as no surprise that individuals will strongly support their associations if these manage to adequately serve their requirements, i.e., if they are satisfied with the results which these associations deliver. To the extent that associations fail to deliver the desired results to individuals, people are apt to withdraw their support and even to act for the break-up and final dissolution of their associations. From this fact we can rightly conclude that: "The first proposition which requires to be brought out into the cold light of the day, and to be kept there remorselessly, at the present time in particular, is that nations are, at bottom, merely associations for the good of those composing them. Please note that I say 'at bottom' ."[138]

The true purpose then of association, of any association, is to maximize the increments of association for each individual to the desired extent possible while simultaneously minimizing to the greatest extent possible the decrements of association for each individual. This is achieved by: 1) efficiently optimizing the advantages that can be gained by the unearned increment of association (i.e., no artificial limits should be imposed) and 2) distributing these advantages in a concretely equitable (but not necessarily equal) manner (this will involve supplying benefits according to that pattern of distribution which shows itself to work best in practice in maintaining a stable and flourishing association).[139] The group and group

---

[137] C.H. Douglas, *The Control and Distribution of Production* (London: Cecil Palmer, 1922), 132.

[138] C.H. Douglas, *The Tragedy of Human Effort* (Vancouver: The Institute of Economic Democracy, 1978), 2. That the 'common good' is to be understood distributively and not collectively, that it is the good of each individual which needs to be promoted to the greatest degree feasible and not the well-being of the whole at the expense of some individual or group of individuals, follows quite logically from the ontological priority which the individual holds over the group. On this understanding, the true purpose of any association is to forward as effectively, as efficiently, and as equitably as possible, the well-being of each one of its individual members in line with the particular types of benefits with which the association deals. Any association can be evaluated in terms of how adequately it satisfies individual requirements on this basis.

[139] In seeking to evaluate any association, we can therefore pose the two following questions: 1) Is the unearned increment of association as great as the membership desires it to be (provided that the desired advantages are objectively feasible)?, and 2) Are the advantages of the unearned increment distributed equitably (not necessarily equally) amongst the membership? The equitable, i.e., correct, pattern of distribution discussed in the second question is a function of what it is that is necessary in order to maximize the unearned increment that was mentioned in the first.

activity should always be regarded as a mere means to the well-being of the sovereign individual and never, in any way, as an end in and of itself.

We have claimed that democratically structured associations which effectively attain their objectives are more stable because they more adequately serve the individual's requirements. The delivery of more satisfactory results is due to the fact that democratic associations have two basic advantages over their despotic counterparts.

In the first place, they successfully subordinate the environment to individuality. The self-development of the individual is, as we have seen, one of the basic purposes of man, but this self-development is dependent on the individual acquiring control over his environment. Human beings who, to the extent that it is physically or objectively possible, are more powerful in shaping their environment than the environment is in shaping them are in a far better position to flourish. They have acquired the type of existential independence which constitutes the most authentic meaning which might be attached to the word 'freedom'. This propitious state of affairs leads quite naturally to greater individual satisfaction with their associations.

In the second place, democratically structured associations are more stable because they successfully bring the policy of the association into full alignment with the policy of the individuals in that association, i.e., they eliminate conflict. So long as the true purpose of the group and its activity is conceived of as facilitating, to the maximum extent, the desires of the individual to achieve his own independent ends (provided that these are compatible with proper group functioning), the interest of the group and the interests of the individuals who compose the group must coincide: "It is most probably true that there can be no divergence between true Public Interest and any true private interest; ..."[140]

Where the policy of an association is to serve the interests of each individual in the best possible way, all must benefit. There is a general interest in the private advantage and a private interest in the general advantage.

By contrast, the alternative forms of association which are based on the opposite policy, i.e., the despotic forms, attempt to subordinate in various ways and to various degrees the individual to the group and hence to the environment. They often sacrifice the genuine interests of the individual in order to advance the specious interests of the group.

---

[140] C.H. Douglas, *Social Credit*, rev. ed. (New York: Gordon Press, 1973), 55.

Associations which frustrate the fulfillment of the basic purpose of self-development in this manner are, to the degree to which they subordinate the individual to the environment, at odds with the objective nature of reality.[141] They disregard the nature of the individual and the fact that, in the final analysis, individuals *only* associate in order to make it easier for them to obtain something that they could not obtain on their own. The resultant frustration of a legitimate drive in man's nature generates dissatisfaction and this dissatisfaction reacts, in various ways, on the structure and functioning of these associations and presages their decay and downfall. Despotic associations suffer from "the well-known phenomena of inefficiency inseparable from the attempted subordination of the human ego to the necessities of a non-human system."[142]

Furthermore, since the overriding policy of a despotic association deviates from the genuine interests of the individuals who make it up, there is a conflict between the aims which the association seeks to actualize and the ends which the sovereign individual would like to achieve. This only intensifies the forces which threaten the continued existence of the association.

The democratic model of association, while it remains authentically and truly democratic, also possesses a third great advantage over the despotic model of association which can help account for its superior stability: the democratic model is not vulnerable in the way that the despotic model is to being taken over by interests that are alien to the true purpose of the association.

It is certainly theoretically possible for an association grounded on the philosophy of external control to operate, to at least some extent, in the best interests of the individuals who compose it. Take, for example, the case of the suitably enlightened benevolent despot. In practice, however, Lord Acton's dictum holds true: "All power tends to corrupt and absolute power corrupts absolutely." Powers of external control centralized in the

---

[141] It is for this reason that Douglas was able to assert that: "Every extension of extraneous control – if you prefer it, of non-immanent sovereignty – is demonstrably against the inherent nature of the human individual, i.e. is contrary to reality." C.H. Douglas, *"Whose Service is Perfect Freedom"* (Bullsbrook, Western Australia: 1983), 40.

[142] C.H. Douglas, *The Control and Distribution of Production* (London: Cecil Palmer, 1922), 44.

hands of the few leads quite automatically, given the weaknesses of human nature, to the establishment of an oligarchy:

> **[I]t appears to be proved beyond argument that Lord Action, in his much misquoted dictum that all power tends to corrupt, and absolute power corrupts absolutely, was enunciating a natural law so that the more powerful a Government is, the more certainly it will deteriorate.**[143]

Now, despotically structured associations which also happen to be oligarchies interfere to an even greater extent with the adequate fulfillment of the true purpose of association because, in addition to subordinating the common individual to the social environment, they also seek to optimize the benefits of association for the elite class that controls the group by maximizing the increments of association while minimizing the decrements of association for that particular group and at the expense of everyone else. This highly inequitable distribution of the unearned increment is achieved by: 1) artificially restricting the advantages that can be had *via* the unearned increment of association and 2) permitting access to this reduced unearned increment only on terms which benefit the oligarchic elite at the illegitimate expense of the common individual members. This type of exploitation only increases the sense of frustration that the individual must experience when forced to operate within such an association.

By contrast, the democratically structured association, because it recognizes "the necessity for exalting the individual over the group",[144] is better placed in principle to prevent an association from sliding under any type of oligarchic control.

For all of these various reasons, Social Credit theory, which stands for "the supremacy of the individual considered collectively, over any external interest",[145] does not hesitate to recognize the democratic model of association as universally normative:

---

[143] C.H. Douglas, *The Development of World Dominion* (Sydney: Tidal Publications, 1969), 71.

[144] C.H. Douglas, *Warning Democracy*, 3rd ed. (London: Stanley Nott, 1935), 74.

[145] C.H. Douglas, *Economic Democracy*, 5th ed. (Sudbury, England: Bloomfield Books, 1974), 28. Ibid., 30-31: "If ... any condition can be shown to be oppressive to the individual, no appeal to its desirability in the interests of external organisation can be considered in extenuation; ..."

[A] nation or other corporate body exists to further the interests of individuals; or, to put it in a more technical form, there is an increment of association derived from the co-operation of individuals, which should be distributed amongst the individuals, if the object of their co-operation is to be achieved successfully.[146]

The Anatomy of Democratically Structured Associations

Democratically structured associations have the potential to deliver the most satisfactory conception of the common good, i.e., the maximization of the net increment of association for each individual to the extent that this is physically or objectively possible, because they respect one aspect of the truth about associations. There are, however, other norms which must also be adhered to if this potential is to be realized in practice. This brings us to a fuller consideration of the correct *principles of association*:

To Social Crediters it is a fairly common-place saying that what we are trying to do with the money system is to make it reflect facts, but what we are also trying to do is to make the relationship between individuals and their institutions reflect facts. To borrow from the Dean of Canterbury's vocabulary, what Social Crediters have in mind is 'to know the truth in order that the truth shall make you free,' ...[147]

Just as there are laws which govern the health of the human body, so too are there laws which govern the well-being of associations. These principles must be incarnated by appropriate mechanisms if any association is to adequately fulfill its true purpose:

The general principles which govern association for the common good are as capable of exact statement as the principles of bridge building, and departure from them is just as disastrous.[148]

---

[146] C.H. Douglas, *Warning Democracy*, 3rd ed. (London: Stanley Nott, 1935), 92.

[147] C.H. Douglas, *The Approach to Reality* (London: K.R.P. Publications Ltd., 1936), 6.

[148] C.H. Douglas, *The Tragedy of Human Effort* (Vancouver: The Institute of Economic Democracy, 1978), 2.

Generally speaking, any activity in association is a function of three component parts: 1) policy, 2) administration, and 3) sanctions: "action on or through an organisation involves three ideas – the idea of policy, the idea of administration, and the idea of sanctions, that is to say, power."[149]

Policy deals with the objective(s) of the association, administration with the system of organization by means of which this objective is carried out, and sanctions with the mechanisms available to the association to ensure that policy and administration, ends and means, are appropriately united.

It is important to recognize that there are two distinct sorts of operating systems by means of which the policy-determining, administration-executing, and sanction-levelling powers can be arranged within the context of an association.

There is, in the first place, the pyramidal type of organization where increasing authority is exercised over larger groups within the association by ever smaller groups until ultimate authority is exercised by the individual or group at the apex of the pyramid. If the larger groups of people do not do as they are told by the smaller groups, the smaller groups have the power to sanction the larger groups up to and including forcing them out of the organization.[150] The alternative type of organization is the circular model of organization where ultimate authority is exercised by the largest group conceivable in the association; i.e., each individual member has power over the smaller groups in the association. In this set up, the common individuals who could be imagined as occupying the circumference of the circle have the power to sanction those smaller groups within the circle if they don't do as they are told, up to and including displacing them from their positions.

Douglas claimed that when the policy-determining, administration-executing, and sanction-levelling powers are properly constituted and arranged, we are able "to work for the right ends in the right way."[151] In other words, associations will be successful if they adopt the right sort of operating systems for the right sort of tasks.

---

[149] C.H. Douglas, *The Tragedy of Human Effort* (Vancouver: The Institute of Economic Democracy, 1978), 3.

[150] In some cases, of course, pyramidal organizations have gone to the extreme of sanctioning individuals by physically or mentally injuring or even killing subordinate actors in the hierarchy.

[151] C.H. Douglas, *Economic Democracy*, 5th ed. (Sudbury, England: Bloomfield Books, 1974), 29.

From the standpoint of a purely theoretical consideration of alternatives, there are four possible paradigms which an association can adopt where operating systems are concerned. These four possibilities are based on the fact that policy can be either democratic or despotic (alongside decentralized or centralized control over sanctions), while administration can be either centralized (hierarchical) or decentralized (anarchic). In other words, when it comes to deciding *what* to do and who is to do it, an association can either be pyramidal or circular. The same fundamental choice arises when attention is turned towards determining *how* things are to be done:

The Four Possible Models of Association

	Despotic Policy /Centralized Sanctions	Democratic Policy /Decentralized Sanctions
Centralized Administration	Category 1	Category 3
Decentralized Administration	Category 2	Category 4

The first possible combination would involve a despotic policy, centralized control over sanctions, and a centralized control over administration. In other words, the pyramidal model of organization is used for determining both what ought to be done and how it ought to be done (as well as who is to do it). Power over both policy and administration are possessed by the apex of a hierarchical social structure. In order to maintain this structure it is crucial that the sanctions are also monopolized by those at the apex; i.e., the individual can have no right to contract out if he does not agree with the policy-decisions of those in control. This arrangement is the type of material structure which is possessed by despotic associations to one extent or another.

The second possible combination would entail despotic policy, centralized control over sanctions, and the decentralized control of administration. It thus combines the pyramidal system where the first task of association is concerned with the circular system for the second task. This option must be discounted as a mere theoretical possibility. Decentralized administration is the negation of any kind of hierarchical structure; anyone can do anything he pleases at any time with respect to the methods of attaining a given objective. No one is ultimately in charge and so there is no structure involving a division of responsibilities and of labour which could ever ensure that a given policy-decision would ever be put into effect. The great inefficiency which characterizes decentralized administration would necessarily prevent an effective association formed in accordance with this model from ever coming into being.

The fourth arrangement, which only employs the circular model of organization, i.e., a democratic policy and decentralized control over sanctions combined with the decentralized control over administration, can also be rejected as a feasible possibility for any successful association for the exact same reason.

This leaves the third combination as the only remaining option. While it is impossible to have an effective and efficient administrative system which is not to some extent hierarchical, it is practically possible, within the functional limits of an association, to combine centralized control over administration with a democratic policy and decentralized control over sanctions. In other words, this third option unites the circular model of organization for determining what ought to be done with the pyramidal model for determining how it ought to be done. This is the specific combination which characterizes *successful* democratically structured associations and, since the democratically structured association has been shown to be the type of association which is best suited to fulfill the true purpose of association, it follows that the third permutation embodies all of the correct principles of association:

That you must have policy democratic and execution hierarchical is one of our fundamental conceptions in Social Credit; ...[152]

---

[152] C.H. Douglas, *The Policy of a Philosophy* (Vancouver: The Institute of Economic Democracy, 1977), 8.

Cf. C.H. Douglas, *Economic Democracy*, 3rd ed. (Sudbury, England: Bloomfield Books, 1974), 39: "it is vital to devise methods by which technical co-ordination can be combined with individual freedom. To crystallize the matter into a paragraph; in respect of any undertaking, centralization is the way to do it, but is neither the correct method of deciding what to do nor the question of who is to do it."

Cf. also C.H. Douglas, *The Control and Distribution of Production* (London: Cecil Palmer, 1922), 34-36: "In any undertaking in which men engage, to paraphrase the ever-green Sir W.S. Gilbert, there are always at least two fundamental aspects which demand recognition before success can possibly be expected to accrue to those engaged in it. These are that there must first be a clear, well-defined policy, which means that every person who has any right to be heard in the matter in hand shall agree to the *results* which he is willing to further with his support. And there must be somewhere resident in the venture some person or persons with expert knowledge as to the technical processes by which those results can be achieved with the materials (using the word in its broader sense) at the disposal of those associated together, and this person must have the confidence of the remainder.

I should like you to observe particularly that certain very important – in fact, quite fundamental – relationships proceed from these simple premises. The genesis of such an association is agreement that a certain result is desirable and a general belief that it can be attained – it is not at all necessary that all of those associated shall know how to attain the result, but it is vital that they shall be satisfied with it. We may imagine this association to be the community. Secondly, the person or persons who "know how," who collectively we may call the producers, who will be empowered by the community to materialise the results of the agreed policy, stand fundamentally and unalterably on a basis of Service – it is their business to deliver the goods to order, not to make terms about them, because it is the basis of the whole arrangement that the general interest is best served by this relationship."

Cf. also C.H. Douglas, *Social Credit*, rev. ed. (New York: Gordon Press, 1973), 35-36: "it is patent that the modern world can only be operated through a liberal use of the group idea. If we are to have great co-operative undertakings, by which alone, so far as we are aware, mankind can be freed from the necessity of devoting the major portion of his day to the acquisition of sufficient food, clothing, and shelter from the weather, there must be a submission by those concerned in such enterprises to a given policy, for instance, of production. This is, of course, common sense, and a matter of common observation, and to the extent that there is a legitimate relation between the group interest thus formed, and the personal interests, is sound in every way. But there are two qualifications which can be made in respect of this submission. The first of these is, in plain English, bound up with the length of time per day or per year during which the submission is necessary, and it has already been observed that the free play of modern science and organisation would, under certain circumstances, tend to reduce this to a small minimum within a short time. The second qualification is involved in the phrase 'freedom of association.' "

The Correct Principles of Association

This third category, which envisages an administrative aristocracy *serving* a democracy of policy, contains the essential recipe for the correct social order. Its three basic principles of association stipulate: 1) the right end of association, 2) the right means, and 3) how the two might be properly integrated so that the common good (distributively considered) can be concretely realized.

1. Policy Must be Democratic – 'The Right End'

The first principle deals with the nature of the policy which any association should serve.[153] As we have already established, the correct end or policy of an association is to fulfill its true purpose: the maximization of the net increment of association for each individual with respect to the specific benefit which the association in question seeks to deliver. This purpose must be the only one which the association can admit as its ultimate end because the failure to pursue it in a single-minded fashion, by diverting resources to other ends, will interfere with the capacity of the association to achieve it to the extent that this fulfillment is physically or objectively possible. Since the true purpose of an association always coincides with the *raison d'être* of an association or the reason why people decided to enter into association in the first place, the true purpose is also the only policy which all individual members could agree on and fully support; it is the only policy which could truly be designated as a *common* policy:

---

[153] Cf. C.H. Douglas, *The Tragedy of Human Effort* (Vancouver: The Institute of Economic Democracy, 1978), 4:

"Now, while no action involving co-operative effort can take place without the presence of these three factors of policy, administration, and sanctions, and therefore they are all essential, and, in a sense, equally important, the first of them in point of time must be policy."

> There is no possible definition of a policy which is all-embracing in its acceptance other than the word "Freedom". People only unite in wanting what they want.[154]

The correct policy of association, being a common policy, is also, therefore, a democratic policy in the truest sense of that word and its acceptance as the governing policy of an association is necessary if an association is to survive and flourish. Douglas insisted that: "a genuine democracy of policy is the fundamental basis of association, and that no association which disagrees with this idea can continue."[155]

2.   Administration Must be Hierarchical – 'The Right Means'

A second necessary condition for a successful association is that the association must employ the best means available for the execution of the correct policy. In contradistinction to the realm of policy, Douglas noted that effective administration *must* be hierarchical and abide by the principle of free association. Administration which embodies a pyramidal structure allows, in comparison with other arrangements, for the efficient and effective concentration of co-operative effort in the pursuit of a well-defined goal:

> In regard to administration, I do not propose to say very much beyond the fact that it is and must be essentially hierarchical and therefore it is a technical matter in which the expert must be supreme and ultimately autocratic ... The idea that administration can be democratic ... is not one which will bear the test of five minutes' experience. It may be consultative, but in the last resort some single

---

[154] C.H. Douglas, *The Control and Distribution of Production* (London: Cecil Palmer, 1922), 37. Cf. C.H. Douglas, *The Tragedy of Human Effort* (Vancouver: The Institute of Economic Democracy, 1978), 12:

"What is important is that we should become conscious of our sovereignty – that we should associate consciously, understanding the purpose of our association, and refusing to accept results which are alien to the purpose of our association."

[155] C.H. Douglas, *Dictatorship by Taxation* (Vancouver: The Institute of Economic Democracy, 1978), 11.

person must decide.[156]

A hierarchical structure allows for a generally recognized and respected division of duties, for rapid decision-making, and for the effective communication of these decisions from the apex to the lower levels. Together, these elements make it far easier to effectively and efficiently carry out a policy-directive:

> [A] centralized or pyramid form of control ... is in certain conditions, the ideal organization for the attainment of one specific and material end. The only effective force by which any objective can be attained is in the last analysis the human will, and if an organization of this character can keep the will of all its component members focussed on the objective to be attained, the collective power available is clearly greater than can be provided by any other form of association.[157]

When this administrative hierarchy is also made subject to the principle of free association, the best people can be selected for specific tasks, thus producing the most effective unit possible for the achievement of those tasks:

> The foundation of successful administration, in my opinion, is that it shall be subject to the principle of free association, which will, in itself, produce in time the best possible form of technical administration. If the conditions of work in any undertaking, and the exercise of authority are ordinarily efficient, and there is in the world any reasonable amount of opportunity of free association, such an undertaking will automatically disembarrass itself of the malcontent, while being obliged to compete for those whose help is necessary to it.
>
> On the other hand, if there is no free association, the natural inertia of the human being and the improper manipulation of methods and

---

[156] C.H. Douglas, *The Tragedy of Human Effort* (Vancouver: The Institute of Economic Democracy, 1978), 4-5.

[157] C.H. Douglas, *Economic Democracy*, 5th ed. (Sudbury, England: Bloomfield Books, 1974), 38.

aims will make an undertaking inefficient, since there is no incentive to reform.[158]

Social Credit's advocacy of centralized control of administration does come, however, with a few caveats.

To begin with, let it not be thought that Social Credit advocates that all administration in a state or in an economy, let us say, should be maximally centralized in one overarching bureaucracy, as is typical in a totalitarian regime. On the contrary, it would be in the interests of efficiency to have several separate and independent administrative hierarchies for different tasks. There is a law of diminishing returns where size is concerned and after a certain point the gains made possible by hierarchical administration can be offset by the bulkiness of the organisation. It is also wise, in keeping with Lord Acton's famous observation that all power tends to corrupt, to distribute the centralized power of administration amongst a variety of many hierarchies so as to lessen the prospects of corruption and monopoly power-wielding.

Secondly, it should be noted that, on Douglas' view, the technique of administration is not a cold empirical science whose principles can be applied rigidly without regard for either the dignity or the personalities of the individuals who make up the administrative hierarchies. Rather, he recognized that administration "is an art, ..." and "is wholly concerned with the satisfactory adjustment of individuality to organisation."[159]

Thirdly, Douglas held that the administrative hierarchies operating in democratically structured associations should be extraordinarily flexible when it comes to the employment of specific administration mechanisms. These should be retained only if and to the extent that they serve the best interests of the individual, precisely because the individual is the proper

---

[158] C.H. Douglas, *The Tragedy of Human Effort* (Vancouver: The Institute of Economic Democracy, 1978), 4-5. Cf. C.H. Douglas, *Credit Power and Democracy* (Melbourne: The Social Credit Press, 1933), 113: "the only claim which any individual or collection of individuals has to *operate* and administer the plant [or, more broadly, the administrative hierarchies – OH] of society is that they are the fittest persons available for the purpose. This can only be the case where there is natural attraction between a man and his work, because no man or woman ever excelled at any pursuit for which they entertained a dislike when in competition with numbers of persons who added to equal capacity an affinity for their occupation."

[159] C.H. Douglas, *The Control and Distribution of Production* (London: Cecil Palmer, 1922), 99.

end of association. What matters is that individuals obtain the results they have a right to expect from their associations:

Systems were made for men, and not men for systems, and the interest of man which is self-development, is above all systems, whether theological, political or economic.

Accepting this statement as a basis of constructive effort, it seems clear that all forms, whether of government, industry or society must exist contingently to the furtherance of the principles contained in it. If a State system can be shown to be inimical to them it must go; if social customs hamper their continuous expansion they must be modified; if unbridled industrialism checks their growth, then industrialism must be reined in. That is to say, we must build up from the individual, not down from the State.[160]

Finally, it is absolutely crucial that administrative hierarchies actually do promote in practice, always, everywhere, and to the best of their ability, the real interests of the individuals composing society. Hierarchical structures and the 'aristocratic' classes who are best able to operate them do not exist for the purpose of domination or for the purpose of imposing a self-serving policy which benefits those in the hierarchy at the expense of the common individual, but exist instead for the purpose of delivering effective *service* to the common individual – a fundamentally Christian idea.

3.   *Sanctions Must be Decentralized – 'The Right Integration between End and Means'*

The only way that correct policy can be introduced and retained by an association is if there is some mechanism or mechanisms in place which can ensure that, should the general *de facto* policy of an association deliver results which are at odds with the true purpose of that association, the individuals who compose that association have the power to bring the activities of the association back into line with the intended results that would be the fruit of a truly *common* policy. In other words, effective sanctions must be possessed by those who are to have control over policy

---

[160] C.H. Douglas, *Economic Democracy*, 5th ed. (Sudbury, England: Bloomfield Publishers, 1974), 29-30.

(power to determine a policy and power to enforce that policy must reside in the same agency if power to select a policy is to equate to power *over* policy) and, in the case of an association which is democratically structured, decentralized control over policy requires decentralized sanctions.[161]

Now it would appear that the most effective sanctions constitute negative forms of control, i.e., individuals should have the ability to atrophy functions which do not serve their best interests. The most powerful sanction of this type would be the right to contract out of any association which failed to serve the individual optimally with no other penalty than the loss of the association itself. The power to opt out in this manner constitutes the death-blow to any oligarchy: "association for the attainment of an objective inevitably becomes a tyranny (*i.e.*, an attack on individual initiative) unless it can be broken at any time, without incurring any penalty other than the loss of association itself."[162]

In one way or another, sanctions must also be made available to the individual members of an association to reprimand or replace head administrators if they cannot or will not serve the common policy in the most effective and efficient manner possible. It is not for the individual member to tell the administrator how to do his job (as the former typically lacks the required technical competency); he should, however, be able to com-

---

[161] Cf. C.H. Douglas, *Economic Democracy*, 5th ed. (Sudbury, England: Bloomfield Books, 1974), 91-92: "Since the analysis of existing conditions which we have undertaken shows that any centralised administrative organisation is certain to be captured by some interest antagonistic to the individual, it seems evident that it is in the direction of decentralization of control that we must look for such alteration in the social structure as would be self-protective against capture for interested purposes." It seems that this lack of adequately decentralized sanctions is one of the single greatest flaws in present social arrangements: "at the present time, there is no question that it is in the domain of sanctions that the human race is involved in its great difficulties." C.H. Douglas, *The Tragedy of Human Effort* (Vancouver: The Institute of Economic Democracy, 1978), 5. Cf. also C.H. Douglas, *The Control and Distribution of Production* (London: Cecil Palmer, 1922), 51: "It has frequently and rightly been emphasised that the essence of any real progress towards a better condition of society resides in the acquisition of control of its functions by those who are affected by its structure; and it is well if somewhat vaguely recognised by the worker of all classes that this control is at present not resident in, but is external to, society itself, and that in consequence men and women, instead of rising to an ever superior control of circumstance, remain the slaves of a system they did not make and have not so far been able to alter in its fundamentals."

[162] C.H. Douglas, *The Control and Distribution of Production* (London: Cecil Palmer, 1922), 101.

municate any lack of satisfaction with the concrete results of the administrator's work in such a way that the administrator will either improve or else lose his privileged position of service to the community.

A General Evaluation of Contemporary Associations

At this point, it would be opportune to bring theory to bear on practice by inquiring whether and to what extent the various associations which populate the world at the present time may actually qualify as successfully democratic models of association.

We have only to consider the unceasing cries of dissatisfaction which are continually voiced from disparate quarters in order to conclude that many of our contemporary associations, whether they be political, economic, or even cultural in nature, are, if not forms of oligarchical collectivism, deviations from the democratic model and that they stifle the full and organic development of the individual:

> **Practically all the evils from which we suffer at the present time can be traced to the ability resident in existing organisations to subordinate true individuality to them. It must be a common experience of many people here to-night to have been obliged to acquiesce passively in transactions either of a business concern or a Government Department which transgress every canon of common decency, and which if done for the advantage of an individual would be generally condemned. The fact that they are done under the orders or for the advantage of some organisation is commonly held to excuse their character.[163]**

---

[163] C.H. Douglas, *Warning Democracy*, 3rd ed. (London: Stanley Nott, 1935), 74. Douglas described the oligarchic structure of economic association in the United Kingdom during the interwar period as follows:

"As a society is at present constituted, it is quite definitely to its advantage, and tends to the perpetuation of the present form of Society, that Lancashire mill operatives should work the maximum number of hours at a very dull occupation, with the minimum of change of work, and if individuals had no interests as such, that is to say, if they were Robots, contemporary society would probably work very well, and no difficulties would arise. But Lancashire mill operatives are developing individualities, and their interests are clearly not the same as those of Society as at present constructed." C.H. Douglas, *Social Credit*, rev. ed. (New York: Gordon Press, 1973), 57.

It must be readily admitted that most contemporary associations fail this basic test of adequacy; i.e., they do not properly serve the interests of their individual members. Instead, by confusing means with ends, they elevate the group to an end in itself to one extent or another and end up treating the individual as a mere means: "A more or less conscious effort to refer the results of the working of the social and political system to the Bar of individual requirement has, on the whole, quite definitely resulted in a verdict for the prosecution; …"[164]

Social Credit Policy with respect to Existing Associations

Given the superiority of the effectively functioning *democratic* model of association, it is clearly in the interests of every individual *qua* individual to exert pressure in favour of the authentic democratization of every association of which he is a part. Associations of all types must be moved away from the totalitarian end of that spectrum which was presented previously and geared towards the democratic ideal: "The pyramidal structure of Society gives environment the maximum control over individuality. The correct objective of any change is to give individuality maximum control over environment."[165]

From this perspective, the *sine qua non* of authentic progress within the domain of association is nothing more nor less than: "the emancipation of the individual from the domination of the group, …".[166]

Totalitarian Structure -- Democratic Structure

The Objective of the Social Credit Movement

---

[164] C.H. Douglas, *Economic Democracy*, 5th ed. (Sudbury, England: Bloomfield Books, 1974), 27. In many, if not in most cases, the failure of associations to embody the proper structure is due to the fact they are subject, in turn, to an economic and financial system which is fundamentally despotic in nature. This particular aspect of the problem has been explored at length in my book, *Social Credit Economics*.

[165] C.H. Douglas, *Economic Democracy*, 5th ed. (Sudbury, England: Bloomfield Books, 1974), 102.

[166] C.H. Douglas, *Warning Democracy*, 3rd ed. (London: Stanley Nott, 1935), 74.

The key goal of the Social Credit movement which Douglas spear-headed was and is to work, by various means, for the reformulation of associations of all types by bringing them into line with the correct principles of association so that the increments of association for each individual can be maximized and the decrements minimized. *It is therefore a movement which unites every individual in a common purpose.* By proceeding in this manner, associations will become far more satisfactory for the individual membership since the former will be in a far better position to fulfill their true purposes with the least amount of trouble to everyone. It is in this sense, above all, that "Social Credit is the policy of a philosophy."[167] Douglas held that this policy is a realistic policy; i.e., "[i]t is something based on ... a portion of reality."[168] Social Credit is not a destructive, revolutionary movement advocating the dissolution of associations or of society in general as a necessary preliminary for their replacement with something better, but is, instead, a constructive, evolutionary movement which seeks to purify existing associations by making them more fully effective. Writing on the state of the political and economic associations of his day, Douglas sketched the changes that were necessary from the point of view of Social Credit policy:

It is suggested that the primary requisite is to obtain in the readjustment of the economic and political structure such control of initiative that by its exercise every individual can avail himself of the benefits of science and mechanism; that by their aid he is placed in such a position of advantage, that in common with his fellows he can choose, with increasing freedom and complete independence, whether he will or will not assist in any project which may be placed before him.[169]

In this connection, it should be re-emphasized that neither the Social Credit theory of association, nor the policy of the Social Credit movement, is, in any sense of the word, 'utopian'. It is not to conform societies to a comprehensive blueprint of what the 'perfect society' is or would be like

---

[167] C.H. Douglas, *The Policy of a Philosophy* (Vancouver: The Institute of Economic Democracy, 1977), 3.

[168] Ibid., 3.

[169] C.H. Douglas, *Economic Democracy*, 5th ed. (Sudbury, England: Bloomfield Books, 1974), 74.

that the Social Credit principles of association are to be respected, rather it is for the sake of freeing individual initiative so that human beings may be enabled to fashion their individual environments in keeping with their own natural proclivities and, ultimately, best interests:

> [S]o far from the realisation of some machine-made Utopia which would embrace us all, I think what we all as individuals desire is a state of affairs which would enable us to use the benefits conferred upon us by science and education for the furtherance of our own individual ideals and desires, which must be just as different, in the nature of things, as our personalities are different, and must become increasingly different as our personalities become further individualised.
>
> The Social Credit proposals at any rate start from this point of view, and in one sense they may be considered as a complete inversion of either State Socialism, Fascism, or Sovietism. So far from desiring to impose some abstract ideal called the "common will' upon the individual, their proposals have for their objective the employment of the common heritage (a phrase which I will define shortly) for the furtherance of the individual objective, whatever that may be, and without defining it.[170]

Far from any question of utopianism, the only alternative to establishing and maintaining an effective democratic association is to disregard in whole or in part the stipulations of the Canon with regard to the structure and functioning of associations. And the consequences of disobeying the Canon in any field of human endeavour are potentially fatal:

> [A]s soon as Society ceases to serve the interests of the individual, then the individual will break up Society ... those persons who wish to preserve Society can do no worse service to their cause, than to depict their idol as an unchangeable organisation whose claims are to be regarded as superior to those of the human spirit.[171]

---

[170] C.H. Douglas, *Warning Democracy*, 3rd ed. (London: Stanley Nott, 1935), 24-25.

[171] C.H. Douglas, *Social Credit*, rev. ed. (New York: Gordon Press, 1973), 73.

An association eventually crumbles whenever the individual is subordinated to the group. Such an arrangement involves treating what is essentially a means as if it were an end in itself, and, as Douglas noted: "It is in the perversion and exaltation of means into ends in themselves, that we shall find the root of our tragedy."[172]

The Chief Mechanism of Oligarchic Hegemony

The Social Credit policy of the full and effective democratization of human associations can only be achieved by neutralizing the main tool which the opposing, oligarchical forces have employed to establish and increase their illegitimate position of domination: the control of communication and hence of information. It must be understood that the control of communication often equates to exercising control over the 'philosophies' or the particular propositional pictures of reality which individuals are likely to accept as true.

If both contemporary and historical associations have deviated from the democratic model of association, it is largely because the oligarchic powers have used their position of privilege to control, through the news media, the educational establishment, and the entertainment industry, etc., how common individuals conceive of reality and how they then interact with reality. The popularization of false pictures of reality allows the Powers-that-be, in various ways, to maintain the subordination of the individual to the group.[173] Douglas referred to this consistent policy of misrepresent-

---

[172] C.H. Douglas, *The Tragedy of Human Effort* (Vancouver: The Institute of Economic Democracy, 1978), 3. Contrary to what the tired mantra of some members of the opposition, i.e., 'there is no alternative', implies, the basic choice, where association is concerned, is not between impossible utopian daydreams and (supposedly) muddling through the best we can, but rather between proper functioning and some type and level of dysfunction. The Social Credit vision of a better society is no more 'utopian' than the reality of physical health: it is achievable through the proper integration of the right ends with the right means. Dysfunction, or indeed ill-heath in any sphere, always seems to involve some sort of imbalance and that imbalance may often be the result of treating means as if they were ends in themselves and true ends as if they were mere means. If it is in our power to resolve the imbalance, then it is also in our power to heal the dysfunction.

[173] Naturally, if one's conception of reality is faulty, the interactions with reality which are guided by that conception must also be faulty and yield unsatisfactory results.

ation as 'black magic', hypnotism, perverted psychology, or abstract-tionism. It is essentially the art of mass mind-control. With respect to the control over information which is exercised by the oligarchic classes, Douglas once made the following remarks:

> They are, in my opinion, assisted to attain and to retain their leadership because of their ability to foster and manipulate a characteristic which is essential to the dominance of the group over the individual. The characteristic which I have in mind is that which I have on various occasions called abstractionism. The theologians call it idolatry.
>
> I should define idolatry as the practice of taking some object or virtue, and without understanding or even trying to understand its true nature, investing it with attributes which do not belong to it. It is, I think, a characteristic of immature intelligence and at first sight would not appear to be a serious matter. But it is, in fact, the very devil.[174]

Some of the things that are widely regarded as true and/or good, and which are neither the one nor the other, are only thus regarded because it serves the interests of the oligarchy controlling an association for those things to be thought of in that way:

> Running through all history like the thread of Ariadne, it is possible to trace a continuous policy which I can only describe as a divorce between things themselves and the description of them. ...
>
> We are beginning to recognise ... that this constant tendency to present a false picture of what is actually going on in the world extends all through our civilisation.[175]

The policy of 'divorcing things from the description of them' comprises two main methods. The first step is to hide or obscure the truth:

---

[174] C.H. Douglas, *Warning Democracy*, 3rd ed. (London: Stanley Nott, 1935), 112.

[175] C.H. Douglas, *Major C.H. Douglas Speaks* (Sydney: Douglas Social Credit Association, 1933), 48.

I have no hesitation in saying that the opposition is concerned to keep from you the truth so that you shall not be able to see the truth even when it is before your eyes. Truth is said to lie at the bottom of a well, and the opposition is concerned with keeping truth at the bottom of the well, and it will do its utmost to see that it does not get out.[176]

This practice of hiding the truth, of keeping it secret, is, in the broadest possible sense of the word, the practice of occultism:

Any serious endeavour to identify the origins of world unrest and war inevitably and invariably leads back to what is loosely called occultism – a word which in itself seems to be almost as widely misunderstood as the matters to which it is applied.

To the average individual, it is mixed up with ghosts, seances, and witches. But, as was pointed out in an admirable letter to *The Social Crediter* of December 20, 1941, this emphasis on the allegedly "supernatural" (itself, a suspect word) is neither justified by the dictionary, which defines "occult" as "that which is secret or hidden", or by the nature of the idea which it expresses, which cannot be static. "Occultism", in fact is simply the reverse of *dis*covery. *Demon est Deus inversus.*

Now, it would appear to be fairly obvious that writing or teaching about things "kept secret or hidden", is not occultism, whatever else it is. It is either *dis*covery (dis-closure) or it is deception.[177]

Once the truth has been successfully concealed, the second step is to present a picture of reality which does not correspond to the way things are, but which will encourage the type of action or omissions which will maintain and strengthen the power of the oligarchic elites. It is the practice of deception for distinct social ends: "When a false picture of something is circulated on a large scale, experience teaches us to look contemplatively at

---

[176] C.H. Douglas, *The Approach to Reality* (London: K.R.P. Publications Ltd., 1936), 6.

[177] C.H. Douglas, *The Big Idea* (Bullsbrook, Australia: Veritas Publishing Company, 1983), 15.

the remedy, ..."[178]

Take, for example, the economic analysis of J.M. Keynes which was used in the post-war period to increase the control which financial institutions held over governments by encouraging an enormous increase in public indebtedness. Douglas described Keynes' analysis as: "a very typical instance of what I am referring to as misrepresentation – a tendency to draw a picture which is not a true picture of things as they are."[179]

This false picture of reality must appear to be plausible in order to be widely accepted; it must be dominated by as many instances as possible of what Alice von Hildebrand has referred to as the 'pseudo-obvious':

Now, the world at the present time, while this order of things continues, is full of things which are put forward as being axiomatic, which are not axiomatic, but at the same time you accept them until you are shocked into consciousness of the foolishness of these things, ...[180]

There are many other tricks that can be applied in order to ensure that a false view of reality will be widely accepted. One of these is to get people to engage in 'group-think' (which is usually not that difficult). Many people seem naturally inclined to make their 'thinking' the function of what others in their milieu 'think' – at the very least it saves them the effort of having to think for themselves. This may also appear to serve the individual's interests by ensuring his security and acceptance by others. Indeed, thinking differently from the group can often put the individual in a very uncomfortable position if the group is intolerant, for whatever reason, of dissent. Many political forces have adopted and continue to adopt forms of messaging that attempt to harness this tendency of human psychology. Writing just after the 1st World War, Douglas noted that the political climate in pre-war Germany and post-war Russia were quite similar in spite of the fact that these were supposed to be two very different types of society. One thing they held in common was their exercises in group-think:

---

[178] C.H. Douglas, *Programme for the Third World War* (Liverpool: K.R.P. Publications Ltd., 1943), 18.

[179] C.H. Douglas, *The Approach to Reality* (London: K.R.P. Publications Ltd., 1936), 7.

[180] C.H. Douglas, *Major C.H. Douglas Speaks* (Sydney: Douglas Social Credit Association, 1973), 85.

It is significant that the arguments voiced from all of these quarters are invariably appeals to mob psychology – "Europe must be saved," "Workers of the World unite," etc. The appeal is away from the conscious-reasoning individual, to the unconscious herd instinct. And the "interests" to be saved, require mobs, not individuals.[181]

A variation on this tactic is to get people to associate themselves, as nationals of a certain country or as members of a particular class, with the powers-that-be. If one can be trained to take a sort of vicarious satisfaction in the exploits of the powerful because the powerful are members of one's country, race, class, or religion, etc., then one is far less likely to criticize or refuse to co-operate with the anti-social policies of the elites. Indeed, depending on the degree of identification one might not even be able to perceive that anything anti-social is going on at all.

Another method of ensuring acceptance of a false view of the world is to use words which have either positive or negative associations in the minds of individuals as pegs with which policies or politicians can be erroneously described so as to produce the desired attraction or repulsion. Labels are, for the masses which cannot or will not think for themselves, infinitely more important than the underlying realities to which the labels should accurately correspond but so often do not: "It is possible so to twist the meaning of words, that policies which result in conditions which are progressively obnoxious to the majority of persons affected by them, can yet obtain a considerable amount of support, by an appeal to high-sounding words such as democracy, justice, and equality."[182]

However it is achieved, if you can get people to accept some propositional picture of reality which is false but nevertheless useful for facilitating their compliance with certain ends, you can get them to more or less willingly embark on a path of misdirected effort which will ever more

---

[181] C.H. Douglas, *Social Credit*, rev. ed. (New York: Gordon Press, 1973), 29. Cf. Ibid., 53-54: "the interest of the blood corpuscle, if it can be imagined to have an interest, is only concerned with the body of which it is a constituent in so far as the continued existence of that body tends towards its own progressive evolution, and the interest of the human individual in society is similar. Any other conception, besides being pharisaical and sentimental, is an invitation to all those influences which stand ready to exploit the individual under cover of such phrases as Public Interest and National Duty."

[182] Ibid., 34.

effectively deliver the unearned increment of association to the oligarchy controlling the society. Like all courses of action, however, such a policy also bears an opportunity cost: it introduces dysfunction into an association and dysfunction is a destructive force: " 'Credit is the substance of things hoped for, *the evidence* of things not seen,' and no stable society can endure on *false* evidence."[183]

Overcoming the dysfunction and the oligarchic elites along with it requires exposing those things which have been kept hidden in an entirely truthful manner. The population needs to be disabused of its many false conceptions regarding the nature of reality if authentic social progress is ever to take place:

[I]t has become clear to me that the difficulties which confront the world's miserable struggles towards sanity, are not in the main intellectual difficulties; they are almost wholly problems of de-hypnotisation.[184]

Of course, one of the most important set of things that has remained hidden is the truth regarding the principles which govern association for the common good. In direct opposition to the prevailing policy of domination, one of the most fundamental ideas of Social Credit is:

[T]hat the first essential of a stable, peaceful and successful society is to get at the truth and to present – not misrepresent – the truth to everyone concerned.[185]

---

[183] C.H. Douglas, *The New and the Old Economics* (Sydney: Tidal Publications, 1973), 3.

[184] C.H. Douglas, *"Whose Service is Perfect Freedom"* (Bullsbrook, Western Australia: 1983), 13. The internet appears to be the appropriate and heaven-sent instrument by means of which the traditional monopoly on the dissemination of information can be effectively broken.

[185] C.H. Douglas, "Money: An Historical Survey", *The Fig Tree* No. 2 (September 1936), 140.

Chapter Five: Social Credit and the 'Philosophy' underlying the Christian Revelation

The specific 'philosophy', in the sense of *Weltanschauung*, which grounds Social Credit is that of Christianity or, more precisely, the general worldview implied by the Christian revelation.[186] Like any other religion, Christianity presupposes in a more or less explicit manner certain beliefs about the nature of the human individual, the nature of the universe, and the place of man in that universe, etc.; i.e., it entails a certain metaphysical, ethical, psychological, historical, and sociological orientation. It is this general orientation which Social Credit shares with Christianity.[187]

Even before undertaking an evaluation of its specific truth-claims, we can already affirm that the Christian *Weltanschauung*, like any other 'philosophy', is either substantially true or else it is not:

It must be insisted that Christianity is either something inherent in the very warp and woof of the Universe, or it is just a set of interesting opinions, largely discredited, and thus doubtfully on a par with many other sets of opinions, and having neither more nor less claim to consideration.[188]

---

[186] It is this shared 'philosophy' that *defines* "the relationship which exists between Social Credit and not only religion but a particular religious system, namely that variously called the Christian or Catholic." Tudor Jones, *Elements of Social Credit* (London: K.R.P. Publications Ltd., 1946), 7. Douglas also remarked that Christianity and Social Credit, together with democracy, have three other points of contact: "Christianity, Democracy, and Social Credit have at least three things in common; they are all said to have failed, none of them is in the nature of a Plan, and every effort of some of the most powerfully organised forces in the world is directed to the end, not only that they never shall be accepted, but that as few persons as possible shall even understand their nature." C.H. Douglas, *"Whose Service is Perfect Freedom"* (Bullsbrook, Western Australia: 1983), 38.

[187] In order to be a Social Crediter, one must therefore be willing to accept, whether or not one is a practising member of this or that Christian denomination, the basic truths of the authentic Christian worldview.

[188] C.H. Douglas, *The Realistic Position of the Church of England* (Liverpool: K.R.P. Publications Ltd., 1948), 12.

One indication of the truth of Christianity may be the fact that so many of the most fundamental distinctions that one can make are three-folded. In writing about the basic

With respect to this question of truth, the fact that the *Weltanschauungen* which underlie both the Christian revelation and Social Credit are one and the same was not purposefully intended by Douglas; rather, Douglas based Social Credit on what showed itself in experience to be real. It was only 'after the fact', as it were, that he realized that the particular *Weltanschauung* which Social Credit presupposed was not a new and unique discovery, but had been present as the implicit basis of the authentic Christian outlook since the very dawn of that particular faith:

> **Social Credit is Christian, not primarily because it was designed to be Christian, but because it was painstakingly "dis"-(un)-covered reality. If Christianity is not real, it is nothing; it is not "true", it *is* Truth.**[189]

Now the general truth of the Christian *Weltanschauung* could be demonstrated, Douglas thought, by observing the success which attended the proper application of its chief principles in the conduct of human life:

> **The whole validity of the Christian Church rests upon the acceptance of certain premises. Those premises are not provable by reason, or they would not be premises. But they *are* provable or disprovable by experience, and to my mind, quite a surprising number of the Christian premises will stand the test.**[190]

Douglas listed two of these premises, perhaps two of the most important premises where Social Credit is concerned, as the claims that "individuals are more important than institutions, and that the end never

---

elements of social action which include philosophy, policy, and mechanism, Douglas observed that: "Like most important matters in the Universe, it appears to have a trinitarian aspect." C.H. Douglas, *The Big Idea* (Bullsbrook, Australia: Veritas Publishing Company, 1983), 58. Is the frequency with which these threefold divisions are found within the created order the signature of the triune Creator-God?

[189] C.H. Douglas, *The Development of World Dominion* (Sydney: Tidal Publications, 1969), 15.

[190] C.H. Douglas, *The Realistic Position of the Church of England* (Liverpool: K.R.P. Pub-lications Ltd., 1948), 15.

justifies the means."[191]

The Social Credit Interpretation of New Testament Texts

The chief principles of the Christian worldview are often presented in the New Testament, and especially in the Gospels, in the form of aphorisms. Perhaps the easiest way to clearly grasp the unity of worldview underlying both the Christian religion and Social Credit is to examine the way in which a large number of these aphorisms easily lend themselves to a Social Credit interpretation. In what follows, I do not wish to suggest that the Social Credit interpretation is necessarily the only or even the primary meaning to be attached to these excerpts from Holy Writ, nor do I wish to imply that the following list is in any way exhaustive:

Philosophy and Policy

1. *I came not to send peace, but a sword.* (Matthew 10:34)[192]

Since policy based on the Christian worldview is incompatible with policy based on anti-Christian worldviews, it is impossible to be a partisan of the Christian worldview and not be placed, given the nature of the world we presently live in, in a state of conflict.

2. *Ye shall know them by their fruits.* (Matthew 7:16)

Provided that the best available means have been employed in their service, the truth-value of philosophies can be judged by the success (or lack thereof) of the policies that are based on them. Of course, the reliability of any such judgement also presupposes that one is in possession of the correct standard of 'success'.

---

[191] C.H. Douglas, *The Big Idea* (Bullsbrook, Australia: Veritas Publishing Company, 1983), 5.

[192] Since Douglas was an Anglican and often cited the Sacred Scriptures as a way of illustrating and underscoring his thinking, the Biblical quotes that are found here are taken from the version of the Bible with which Douglas would have been most familiar, i.e., the King James version.

3.   *Do men gather grapes of thorns, or figs of thistles? Even so every good tree bringeth forth good fruit; but a corrupt tree bringeth forth evil fruit.* (Matthew 7:16-17)

It is impossible for truly satisfactory policies to come from false philosophies; a bad tree does not and indeed cannot bring forth good fruit.

Philosophy of Human Nature

4.   *In my Father's house are many mansions:* ... (John 14:2)

Christ indicated that there are many mansions in his Father's house because there are so many different sorts of people. In other words, Christianity, like Social Credit, acknowledges that when it comes to attributes and abilities, there is no ontological equality. However, since there are many mansions, no one need feel excluded or marginalized on account of their specific differences and corresponding inequalities.

The Canon

5.   *My kingdom is not of this world:* ... (John 18:36)

Christianity and Social Credit both recognize "the primacy and formative nature of *ideas.*"[193] We cannot act in a consistent let alone effective manner without having some *idea* as to what it is we are trying to achieve.

6.   *Heaven and earth shall pass away, but my words shall not pass away.* (Matthew 24:35)

The Canon comprises, *inter alia*, certain necessary and universal truths which may be taken as manifestations of the absolute:

---

[193] C.H. Douglas, *The Realistic Position of the Church of England* (Liverpool: K.R.P. Publications Ltd., 1948), 10.

The philosophy of Christianity, as I apprehend it, contends for certain immutable principles which may have many permutations ...[194]

7. *... for the letter killeth, but the spirit giveth life.* (2 Cor. 3:6)

It is very important when dealing with the principles of the Canon to not
mistake the form for the substance. While the principles themselves are, at
their highest levels, immutable, the various ways in which they can be
applied are subject to change depending on differing circumstances. To
hold on to a system or mechanism which was once useful but which is no
longer applicable on account of other developments is to fall into the trap
of the deductive habit of mind, i.e., the subordination of reality to thought,
of facts to theory:

It is not too much to say that one of the root ideas through which
Christianity comes into conflict with the conceptions of the Old Testament and the ideals of the pre-Christian era, is in respect of this
dethronement of abstractionism. That is the issue which is posed by
the Doctrine of the Incarnation.[195]

8. *But seek ye first the kingdom of God, and his righteousness; and all these
things shall be added unto you.* (Matthew 6:33)

If we wish to act correctly we must concern ourselves first and foremost
with discovering the prescriptions of the Canon with respect to the particular field of endeavour in which we wish to act and once they are
known we must obey those prescriptions:

I am confident that single-mindedness of purpose directed to the pursuit of this canon to which I have referred is the only thing of
absolutely primary importance in any undertaking. Given that, forms
of organisation and other mechanisms for the attainment of the end,
necessary as they undoubtedly are, will, as one might say, provide
themselves both at the right time and in the most perfect form that

---

[194] Ibid., 13-14.

[195] C.H. Douglas, *Social Credit*, rev ed. (New York: Gordon Press, 1973), 22.

the necessities of the case require.[196]

The single-minded pursuit of the Canon does not mean that things of this world have no value: "Christianity ... does not scorn this world".[197] Provided that one puts first things first, one is truly free to enjoy whatever good things the world has to offer:

> **It is not improper to say that Christianity is *inter alia* a technique by which a man, by control of his ideation, may gain such part of the world as in the nature of things appertains to him, and there is no injunction of which I am aware against that. But there is a warning. "What shall it profit a man, if he gain the *whole* world, and lose his own soul?"[198]**

> 9.   *For what shall it profit a man, if he shall gain the whole world, and lose his own soul?*(Mark 8:36)

Whenever a person seeks to go beyond what appertains to him in the nature of things he is guilty of a serious ontological transgression and the price of such a rebellion is the loss of his own moral integrity.

> 10.   *Thy kingdom come. Thy will be done in earth, as it is in heaven.* (Matthew 6:10)

Any action undertaken on this earth must be brought into line with the ultimate nature of the universe as specified by the Canon if it is to be ultimately successful.

> 11.   *Even so faith, if it hath not works, is dead, ...* (James 2:17)

The Canon cannot be incarnated without appropriate *action*:

---

[196] C.H. Douglas, *Major C.H. Douglas Speaks* (Sydney: Douglas Social Credit Association, 1933), 53.

[197] C.H. Douglas, *The Realistic Position of the Church of England* (Liverpool: K.R.P. Publications Ltd., 1948), 10.

[198] Ibid., 10.

It is a matter of no consequence whatever that a large number of people *believe* in the truth of Social Credit. The question is – what are they going to do about it?[199]

12. *For my yoke is easy, and my burden is light.* (Matthew 11:30)

Living in keeping with the Canon, in alignment with reality, actually represents the *easiest* way to achieve intended results. Any other approach is simply a waste of effort:

So far as I understand Christianity, it is the easy (not necessarily the immediately easy) way – e.g., the proper way – to do things – "my yoke is easy, my burden, light." It is not a pathetic and everlasting effort to do the undoable. The Satanic ideology of work, employment, austerity, sacrifice, is not an ideology of achievement. Surely anyone can see that. It is an ideology of sabotage, destruction, corruption and decay.[200]

Social Philosophy

13. ... *for, behold, the kingdom of God is within you.* (Luke 17:21)

All social power arises from within each individual and not from without, i.e., from sources of external control:

[O]ne of the fundamentals of genuine Christianity is that the only true focus of power is the individual, which is simply a matter-of-fact method of affirming the Immanence of God over the Monotheistic Jehovah.[201]

---

[199] C.H. Douglas, *The Approach to Reality* (London: K.R.P. Publications Ltd., 1936), 12.

[200] C.H. Douglas, *The Big Idea* (Bullsbrook, Australia: Veritas Publishing Company, 1983), 66-67.

[201] C.H. Douglas, *Programme for the Third World War* (Liverpool: K.R.P. Publications Ltd., 1943), 43.

14. But he that is greatest among you shall be your servant. (Matthew
   23:11)

All positions of administrative authority in an association are positions
of service. They exist to promote the common good and ought never to be
regarded as a point of leverage for the self-serving usurpation of the
unearned increment of association.

15. The sabbath was made for man, and not man for the sabbath: ... (Mark
   2:27)

Just as the sabbath was instituted for the benefit of man and not man for
the sake of the sabbath, all political, economic, and cultural systems are
also in place for the sake of man and should be evaluated and retained
only to the extent that they serve his well-being. To treat systems as ends
in themselves and man as a means to their establishment and expansion is
an inversion of the due order:

> **Systems were made for men, and not men for systems, and the in-
> terest of man which is self-development, is above all systems, wheth-
> er theological, political or economic.**
>
> **Accepting this statement as a basis of constructive effort, it seems
> clear that all forms, whether of government, industry or society must
> exist contingently to the furtherance of the principles contained in it.
> If a State system can be shown to be inimical to them it must go; if
> social customs hamper their continuous expansion they must be
> modified; if unbridled industrialism checks their growth, then in-
> dustrialism must be reined in. That is to say, we must build up from
> the individual, not down from the State.**[202]

---

[202] C.H. Douglas, *Economic Democracy*, 5th ed. (Sudbury: Bloomfield Publishers, 1974), 29-30.

*16. Render therefore unto Caesar the things which are Caesar's; and unto
       God, the things that are God's* (Matthew 22:21)

A successful society will embody one of the key principles of Ramiro de
Maeztu's functionalism: every authority must operate within clearly and
correctly defined limits and no authority should have any more power or
privilege than is necessary for the adequate carrying out of its due function
in favour of the common good. "An expert is essentially a servant of
policy, and we all know what comes of 'a servant when he ruleth'."[203] It
must also be possible to hold every authority personally responsible for
the use of the powers entrusted to him.

The Principle of the Incarnation

After considering these basic premises an obvious question imposes itself: if the worldview underlying Christianity is true, why is it often
claimed that Christianity has failed? Douglas made a startling contribution
both to the future betterment of civilization and to the survival and ultimate vindication of the Christian religion when he pointed out that what
is, perhaps, the most important principle of the Christian worldview is all
too often neglected: *And the Word was made flesh* (John 1:14); it is the truth
taught by the doctrine of the incarnation. The worldview of Christianity
must be applied through proper *mechanisms* if the truth of that worldview
is to be effective in securing worthwhile results on the practical plane:

**The speech of the Earl of Darnley in the House of Lords on July 10,
1946, affords an outstanding instance of a little recognised, but formidable problem. Perfect in form and manner, it was a moving
appeal for the replacement of Power Politics by the Christian Ethic
and the Golden Rule. Where, it may be asked, is there any problem in
that, other than one of wholesale conversion? Let us, in order to elu-
cidate the difficulty, compare Christianity to the Theory of Thermo-
Dynamics, and assume, for the purposes of the argument, that all the
essentials of that theory were widely known two thousand years ago.**

---

[203] C.H. Douglas, *The Tragedy of Human Effort* (Vancouver: The Institute of Economic Democracy, 1978), 9.

It is not difficult to imagine that those who grasped the implications of it might say "Here is the key to a better society. Here is the title deed to a leisure world. Disregard all else, and apply thermody-namics." Remember that we are assuming that James Watt was still to be born. And the world at large would have said "This man says the magic word is Thermo-Dynamics. Crucify him."

Now the fact, which ought to be patent to anyone, is that it is the Policy of a Philosophy which is important (because it is the *evidence* of things not seen); and that Thermo-Dynamics means nothing with-out Heat Engines, and Christianity means nothing without the Incar-nation. You cannot drive a dynamo with Boyle's law, or the "Queen Elizabeth" with Joule's Equivalent. This country is not now the Pol-icy of a Christian Philosophy, and before it can again, as an organi-sation, put into practice *successfully* those Christian principles, for which Lord Darnley pleads, it must understand their application through proper mechanisms – not so simple a matter as he would appear to think it is. Failing that, "the children of this world are, *in their generation*, wiser than the children of Light." [204]

Christian principles must find their expression in the policies and methods that individuals and associations adopt so that reality's inherent potential for goodness might be released and the divine plan for creation fulfilled. Barring this, no amount of sentimental rhetoric, public appeals, ceremonies, and campaigns, or even prayer will succeed, by themselves, in ensuring that the divine will can and shall be done here on earth as it is in heaven. Seeking, respecting, and obeying the Canon in all morally sound fields of human endeavour is one of the greatest forms of divine worship as it renders manifest something of the divinity in this world of time and space ... 'And the Word was made flesh'.

---

[204] C.H. Douglas, *The Development of World Dominion* (Sydney: Tidal Publications, 1969), 20-21.

Antitheses to the Christian Worldview

Another method of throwing light on the content of the Christian worldview, and hence the 'philosophy' which serves as the basis for Social Credit, is to identify what that worldview is not. There are a number of anti-Christian worldviews that are active in the modern world and they, in various combinations and to various degrees, have thoroughly displaced Christianity as the foundational 'philosophy' for public policy. If the authentic Christian *Weltanschauung* is substantially true, then alternatives which deny any of its basic premises must be false:

> **I believe the whole philosophy of the modern world is essentially unreal. Never before have we been going through such an orgy of calculated delusions raised upon a conception, which is consciously vicious, of what is important to the world; and up to a certain extent it succeeds.**[205]

The anti-Christian worldviews which Douglas regarded as false or 'unreal' go by various names in his writings: 'collectivism', 'dialectical materialism', 'freemasonry', 'Puritanism', 'Calvinism', 'Whiggism', 'Prussianism', '(Talmudic) Judaism', etc.

There can be no hope of combining the Christian religion and the worldview it inspires with any anti-Christian religion or worldview and no hope of combining financial, economic, political, and cultural policies that are consonant with Christianity with those that stem from anti-Christian sources.

> **Both philosophies [i.e., the Christian and the anti-Christian - OH] have a policy and these policies cannot live together. The Founder of Christianity was quiet unequivocal on the question. "I came not to bring peace, but a sword."[206]**

Since Social Credit is grounded on what is, in fact, a Christian basis, it must be clearly understood that Social Credit philosophy and Social Credit

---

[205] C.H. Douglas, *The Policy of a Philosophy* (Vancouver: The Institute of Economic Democracy, 1977), 15.

[206] C.H. Douglas, *The Development of World Dominion* (Sydney: Tidal Publications, 1969), 16.

policy are fundamentally at odds with both collectivistic methods of organizing society (e.g., communism, fascism, socialism, and National Socialism, etc.) *and* with their ostensible opposites that are grounded in an excessive and/or disordered individualism (e.g., anarchism, libertarianism, classical liberalism, and neo-liberalism, etc.).

Bibliography

Butler, Eric D. *The Essential Christian Heritage*. Flesherton, Ontario: The Canadian League of Rights, 1971.

—. *Releasing Reality*. Melbourne: Heritage Publications, 1979.

—. *Social Dynamics*. Fitzroy, Australia: W. & J. Barr Pty. Ltd., n.d.

Byrne, L. Denis. *The Nature of Social Credit*. Edmonton: The Social Credit Board, n.d.

Colbourne, Maurice. *The Meaning of Social Credit*. 4th ed. Edmonton, Alberta: The Social Credit Board, 1935.

De Maeztu, Ramiro. *Authority, Liberty and Function in the Light of the War*. London: George Allen & Unwin LTD, 1916.

De Maré, Eric. *A Matter of Life or Debt*. Bullsbrook, Australia: Veritas Publishing Company Pty. Ltd., 1985.

—. "What is Social Credit?" supplement, *The Sun*, no. 15 (Summer 1955).

Dobbs, Geoffrey. "The Douglas Legacy" http://www.alor.org/Library/Dobbs%20G%20%20The%20Douglas%20Legacy.htm

—. *What is Social Credit?* Sudbury, England: Bloomfield Books, 1981.

Douglas, C.H. *The Approach to Reality*. London: K.R.P. Publications Ltd., 1936.

—. *The Big Idea*. Bullsbrook, Western Australia: Veritas Publishing Company Pty. Ltd., 1983.

—. *The Breakdown of the Employment System*. Vancouver: The Institute of Economic Democracy, 1979.

—. *The Brief for the Prosecution*. Liverpool: K.R.P. Publications Ltd., 1945.

—. *The Control and Distribution of Production*. London: Cecil Palmer, 1922.

—. *Credit-Power and Democracy*. Melbourne: The Social Credit Press, 1933.

—. *The Development of World Dominion*. Sydney: Tidal Publications, 1969.

—. *Dictatorship by Taxation*. Vancouver: The Institute of Economic Democracy, 1978.

—. *Economic Democracy*. 5th ed. Sudbury, England: Bloomfield Books, 1974.

—. *Major C.H. Douglas Speaks*. Sydney: Douglas Social Credit Association, 1933.

—. "Major Douglas at Dunedin (N.Z.)." *The Social Credit Standard*, no. 9 (July-August, 1934): 1-12.

—. "Money: An Historical Survey." *The Fig Tree*, no. 2 (September 1936): 139-147.

—. *The Monopolistic Idea*. Vancouver: The Institute of Economic Democracy, 1979.

—. *The Monopoly of Credit*. 4th ed. Sudbury, England: Bloomfield Books, 1979.

—. *The Nature of Democracy*. Vancouver: The Institute of Economic Democracy, 1978.

—. *The Policy of a Philosophy*. Vancouver: The Institute of Economic Democracy, 1977.

—. *Programme for the Third World War*. Liverpool: K.R.P. Publications Ltd., 1943.

—. *Realistic Constitutionalism*. London: K.R.P. Publications Ltd., 1947.

—. *The Realistic Position of the Church of England*. London: K.R.P. Publications Ltd., 19.

—. *Security: Institutional and Personal*. Liverpool: K.R.P. Publications Ltd., 1945.

—. *Social Credit*. London: Cecil Palmer, 1924.

—. *Social Credit*. rev. ed. New York: Gordon Press, 1973

—. *These Present Discontents and The Labour Party and Social Credit*. London: Cecil Palmer, 1922.

—. *The Tragedy of Human Effort*. Vancouver: The Institute of Economic Democracy, 1978.

—. *The Use of Money*. Liverpool: K.R.P. Publications Ltd., 1934.

—. *Warning Democracy*. 3rd ed. London: Stanley Nott, 1935.

—. *"Whose Service is Perfect Freedom."* Bullsbrook, Western Australia: Veritas Publishing Company Pty. Ltd., 1983.

Finlay, John. *Social Credit: the English Origins*. Montréal and London: McGill-Queen's University Press, 1972.

Hattersley, J.M. *Study Course in Social Credit*. http://albertamoneytalk.blogspot.ca/2009/04/study-course-in-social-credit-by-jm.html.

Heydorn, M. Oliver. *The Economics of Social Credit and Catholic Social Teaching*. Ancaster, Ontario: Createspace, 2014.

—. *Social Credit Economics*. Ancaster, Ontario: Createspace, 2014.

Hughes, John W. *Major Douglas – The Policy of a Philosophy*. Edmonton, Alberta: Brightest Pebble Publishing, 2004.

[Jones, Tudor]. *Elements of Social Credit*. London: K.R.P. Publications Ltd., 1946.

Kierkegaard, Søren. *Concluding Unscientific Postscript to Philosophical Fragments*, revised edition. Princeton: Princeton University Press, 1992.

Monahan, Bryan W. *An Introduction to Social Credit*, 2nd ed. London: K.R.P. Publications Ltd., 1967.

Orwell, George. *1984*. New York: Plume, 1983.

Von Hildebrand, Alice. *"On the Pseudo-Obvious"* in *Wahrheit, Wert und Sein : Festgabe fur Dietrich von Hildebrand zum 80. Geburtstag*, ed. Balduin Schwarz Regensburg : Josef Habbel, 1970.

Von Hildebrand, Dietrich. *What is Philosophy?* London and New York: Routledge, 1991.

Walsh, John. *This is Catholicism*. Garden City, New York: Image Books, 1959.

Index

Absolute Idealism, 3
abstractionism, 94, 103
achievement, 24, 105
Acton, Lord, 76, 86
administration, 27, 34, 38, 79, 80, 81,
    83n, 84, 85, 86
    definition of, 28
    relation of administration to
    philosophy, 28-31
Aickman, Robert Fordyce, 15n
alcoholic products, 54
altruism (-tic), 20, 20n
Anamnesis, 6
anarchism, 110
the anti-Canon, 38n
a posteriori, 36
a priori, 36, 46n
Aquinas, Thomas, 2n
Ariadne, 39
Aristotle, 2n
asha, 37n
association (s), vii, xiv, xv, 13, 14, 16,
    16n, 17, 24, 25, 28, 35, 38, 40, 53, 63,
    94, 97, 98, 106, 108
  anatomy of democratically
    structured, 78-82
  correct principles of,
    83-89
  correct purpose of, 73-78
  decrement(s) of, 64, 68, 69, 74, 91
  different types of, 66-72
  evaluation of forms of, 72-78
  freedom of, 82n, 84
  general evaluation of
    contemporary, 89-90
  the general nature of, 64-65
  increment(s) of, 64, 68, 69, 74, 74n
  77, 78, 83, 91, 98
  the philosophies behind, 65-66

Social Credit policy with respect
    to, 90-93
Athanasius, 52
Augustine, 2n, 6

Bacon, Sir Francis, 41, 45, 46n
Bismark, 7
Boethius, 2
Butler, Eric, 27, 30, 32

Calvinism, 109
Canon, the, 36, 37, 37n, 38, 38n, 39,
    40, 40n, 41, 44, 48, 49, 50, 59, 64,
    66n, 92, 102, 103, 104, 105, 108
catholic, 19n, 99n
Catholicism, 49
centralization of power, 69-70
Chesterton, G.K., 40
Christian, 19, 20, 45, 49, 54n, 87, 99n,
    109, 110
the Christian revelation, 13, 21n, 99
    Social Credit and 99-110
Christianity, 99, 100, 102, 103, 104,
    105, 107, 108, 109, 99n, 100n
circular model of organization, 80, 81
collectivism, 15, 109
    oligarchical, 68, 89
common good, 73, 78, 83, 98, 106, 107
    the collectivistic understanding
    of, 73, 74n
    the distributistic understanding
    of, 73, 74n, 83
communism, 110
compulsion, 70, 70n
conventional law 29, 30

Darnby, Earl of, 107, 108

113

Darwin, 11
decentralization of power, 69-70
De Maeztu, Ramiro, 107
De Maré, Eric, 72
Descartes, 6
despotism, 65, 68, 69
determinism, 5, 17n
the devil, 51, 54, 54n, 94,
diversity, 17, 59
Dobbs, Geoffrey, 54n
Douglas, Major Clifford Hugh, vii,
    ix, x, xi, xiii, xiv, xv, 1, 3, 3n, 4, 6,
    7, 8, 9n, 10, 15n, 16, 16n, 17, 19,
    19n, 20, 20n, 21, 25, 26, 27, 29, 32,
    32n, 34, 35, 35n, 36, 37n, 44, 47,
    47n, 48, 49, 50, 50n, 51, 53, 54, 54n,
    56, 57, 59, 60, 60n, 63n, 64, 70n,
    72n, 73, 76n, 79, 84, 86, 89n, 91,
    93, 94, 96, 99n, 100, 100n, 107,
    107n, 109

Economic Democracy, ix
*The Economics of Social Credit and
    Catholic Social Teaching*, ix
eidetic analysis, 1, 1n
empiricism, 6, 8, 10, 46n
England, 5, 45, 54
equality, 15, 15n, 16, 52, 97, 102
Europe, 34, 58, 97
evil, 18, 19n, 31n, 38n, 51, 52, 53, 53n,
    54, 54n, 55, 89, 102
Existentialism, 3n

family, 26, 67n
Faraday, 7
fascism, 92, 110
financial system, 90n
Finlay, John, 20n
First World War, 34
Firth of Forth, 34

the French Revolution, 9n
free will, 13, 13n, 14, 37n, 51n
freedom, 6, 15n, 24, 24n, 50, 66, 66n,
    67, 68, 70, 70n, 75, 82n, 84, 91
freemasonry, 109
frustration, 24, 76, 77
functional necessity(-ies), 16, 65, 66n,
    70

Germany, 96
God, 3n, 6, 21n, 25, 37, 39, 49, 50, 51,
    54, 54n, 55, 58, 66, 100n, 103, 105,
    107
the Golden Rule, 107
the Gospels, 101
Göttingen, ix, 7
group-think, 96

Heydorn, Oliver, ix
hierarchy, 65, 79n, 85, 87
Human life, 21, 26, 49, 50, 53n, 100
    the ultimate end of, 21, 21n, 22, 49
    value of, 26
Human nature, 13, 15, 18, 18n, 19,
    19n, 20, 22, 23, 49, 71, 72, 102
    Basic Goodness of, 19
    Heredity as one of the Chief Roots
        of Inequality of, 17-18
    Inequality of, 15-17
    Root Motive of, 20
    Social Credit view of, 13-15
Husserl, Edmund, ix, 43

idealism, 4, 15n
idolatry, 10n, 94
immorality, 51n
Incarnation, doctrine of, 103
    principle of, 107-108
individuality, 14, 16, 21, 49, 70, 86,
    89, 90

inducement, 70, 70n
inequality (-ties), 15, 16, 16n, 17, 17n,
    18, 18n, 23, 102
Ingarden, Roman, x, xn
initiative (creative, personal,
    individual, etc.), 13, 14, 24, 76 ,88,
    92
innate ideas, 6
intellectualism, 8
International Academy of
    Philosophy, vii, xi

John Paul II, xn, xi
Jones, Dr. Tudor, 11, 99n
Judaism (talmudic), 109

kabbalistic, 35n, 54n
Keynes, J. M., 96
Kierkegaard, 3n
Klinck, Wally, vii

Lancashire, 89n
liberalism, classical, 110
libertarian, 66
libertarianism, 110
logic, 8, 9n, 10n, 45
London, xiii, 34
Lucifer, 9n

materialism, 4, 15, 38n, 52, 109
metanoia, 41
metaphysics, 6
moral progress, 24, 25, 58
morality,
    nature of, 48-55
    vs. moralism, 56-57
    and power, 59
    and progress, 57-58
Munich, 7

Napoleon, 7
National Socialism, 110
natural law, 29, 77
natural science, 5, 10
neo-liberalism, 110
New Testament, xi, 101
North America, 58

occultism, 95
Old Testament, 103
oligarchy, 77, 88, 94, 98
opt out,
    the power to, 88
Orientierungsphilosophie, 2
Original sin, 19, 19n
Orwell, 68
the ought, 5, 31, 32n, 33n, 34n, 35n,
    36, 39, 43, 48, 56, 57, 60, 61, 71
    the nature of (the idealistic vs. the
    realistic ought), 32-36

pacifists, 39
peace, 73n, 101, 109
personalism, xi
phenomenological realism, vii, ix, x
Philosophia Perennis, 2, 2n, 8
philosophy, iii, vii, ix, x, xi, xii, xiii,
    xiv, xv, 1, 2, 4, 13, 27, 63, 64, 66, 72,
    76, 102, 105, 110
'philosophy' 1, 2, 7, 28, 29, 30, 31, 32
    57, 60, 65, 65n, 66, 66n, 72, 93, 99,
    99n, 109
Pinwill, Chas., vii
Poland, xi
policy, vii, 17, 22, 27, 28, 28n, 31n, 32,
    38, 38n, 39, 54, 55, 56, 59, 60, 61,
    62, 64, 66, 67, 69, 75, 76, 79, 80, 81,
    82n, 83, 83n, 84, 85, 87, 88, 90, 91,
    93, 94, 98, 100n, 101, 107, 108, 109,
    110
    definition of, 27

of domination, 66, 98
of freedom, 66, 67
relation of to philosophy, 28-31
Plato, 2n, 6
private interest, 75
Prussianism, 109
psychology, 70n, 94, 96, 97
public interest, 75, 97n
Puritanism, 19n, 109
pyramidal model of organization, 79,
    79n, 80, 81, 84

rationalism, ix, 6, 8, 10, 9n
rationality, 10, 13, 14, 70
realism, 3, 3n, 4, 4n
    epistemological, 3
    metaphysical, 3
    methodological, 3
    philosophical, 3
realist phenomenology, vii, 1n, 7, 8,
    8n
reason, 6, 8, 9, 9n, 10n,
    21, 21n, 237, 43, 100
Reinach, Adolf, x, xn
reincarnation, 17n
religion, 37n, 60n, 97, 99, 99n, 100,
    101, 107, 109
    and the application of the canon,
    59-62
Russia, 96
Russian, 52, 18n

sabbath, 106
Saint John,
    Gospel of, 37
sanctions, 79, 80, 81, 83n, 87, 88, 88n
Satan, 9, 54n
Schroeder, Jim, 3n
Seifert, Dr. Josef, vii, xn, xii, 8n
self-development, 21, 22, 23, 24, 26,
    48, 49, 50, 50n, 55, 75, 76, 87, 106
self-expression, 23, 50
self-interest, 20, 22

self-preservation, 22,23
selfishness, 20
servility, 69
Social Credit, ii, vii, ix, ixn, xi, xiii,
    xiv, 1, 2, 3, 3n, 4n, 13, 18n,
    21, 24 ,25, 27, 38, 40, 53, 61, 63,
    63n, 64, 66n, 77, 81, 86, 90, 91 ,92,
    93, 93n, 98, 99, 99n, 100, 101, 102,
    105, 109, 110
Social Credit Economics, ix, 90n
Social Credit Secretariat, 4,
Social Crediter, xiii, 3n, 27, 72, 78,
    95, 100n
The Social Crediter, 4, 95
social philosophy, 63, 64, 72, 105
socialism, 92, 110
Socrates, 2n, 41n
Solidarność, xi
sovereignty, 55, 66, 69, 84n
    non-immanent, 76n
Sovietism, 92
Spencer, Herbert, 10
Stein, Edith, x
Stephenson, George, 7
subsidiarity, 55n

theosophy, 35n, 54n
totalitarian, 3, 20, 22, 53, 68, 86, 90
totalitarianism, 20, 68
truth, 1, 2, 4n, 6, 7, 16, 30, 31, 35, 37,
    37n, 40, 40n, 41-48, 41n, 46n, 59,
    71, 78, 94, 95, 98, 99n, 100, 100n,
    101, 102, 105, 107
    phenomenological criterion for
    the discernment of, 43-44, 47
tyranny, 39, 88

universe, iii, 2, 3, 9, 15, 30, 31, 31n
    35n, 36n, 37, 37n, 39, 40, 47, 51n,
    53, 61n, 99, 100n, 104
Utopia, 92

von Hildebrand, Alice, 96
von Hildebrand, Dietrich, x, xn, xii, 8

Waite, Will, vii
war, 39
Washington, 7
Watt, James, 7, 108
Weltanschauung, 1 , 2, 99, 100, 109
Wenisch, Fritz, 8n
Whig (Whiggism), 56, 109
Whittaker, Sir Edmund, 10
worldview, 1, 2, 35n, 38, 101, 107,
    109

Zoroastrianism, 37

Made in the USA
Charleston, SC
02 June 2016